I0140471

Thicker *than* Water

Roy Morris

aventine press

Published by Aventine Press
55 East Emerson St.
Chula Vista CA 91911
www.aventinepress.com

ISBN: 978-1-59330-843-8

Library of Congress Control Number: 2013922180
Library of Congress Cataloging-in-Publication Data
Thicker Than Water/ Roy Morris
Printed in the United States of America

Acknowledgements

Without the help, support, encouragement and love of my family and friends, I could not have written this book and even if they are the only ones who buy a copy, each of them will know how much I appreciate their input, their efforts and their contributions.

Within these pages are some stories that I wrote simply because I thought the events just had to be chronicled somewhere. There are some items written in college because of impromptu assignments by my instructors. There are articles which were originally written for publication in one or more of the local newspapers. And there are poems and songs that practically wrote themselves, the words spilling out of my head so fast, I could hardly keep up typing them out.

I hope you will experience the same emotions I felt when I wrote these stories, articles, poems and songs. If you say "Hmmm" over the serious parts, if you marvel over the inspirational parts, if you smile-or even laugh out loud-at the funny parts, and if you get misty-eyed, or maybe even cry, over the sad parts, then I will have had at least a small measure of success as a writer.

I wrote about the things that are near and dear to my heart. I wrote about the people I know and love the best-my family and my friends--and of course, myself. All my life, I have wanted to write The Great American Novel but with this effort, I think I have done something even better. I have written a Novel about some Great Americans.

Thicker Than Water

Roy Morris

Rural Route Three

Chapter 1

Family Matters

We were just poor folks. Ordinary country people. Not much more than hillbillies. Arkansas hillbillies, to be exact (I understand there are hillbillies from other states but they are probably inferior models). To the best of my knowledge, Mom and Dad never owned any land or a house. We lived in rental houses, sometimes with relatives in their rental houses, sometimes in sharecroppers' shacks. And occasionally, we lived in a car or under a tree by the roadside.

Steve and Alta Laverne Morris had seven children. I don't know how they managed to keep us fed and watered long enough to get us raised. Dad was generally a farm laborer and sawmill worker. He did the hardest, dirtiest jobs that had to be done. We were always the poorest family in whatever neighborhood we were part of. During the 50's and 60's, our family lived under the same conditions that poor people had lived under during the 20's and 30's. We lived in houses that did not have electricity or running water. We used kerosene lamps for nighttime illumination. We heated our house with wood-burning stoves and our meals were cooked on wood-burning cook stoves. We used outhouses and took baths in huge galvanized tubs, except in summertime, when we most often bathed in creeks and streams. However, there were also times when I actually broke the ice at the edge of a stream to wade out and do my bathing. I was a tough little rascal

Dad was born in December 1919 in Arkansas and spent most of his life here, hardly ever leaving the state except when he "rode the rails" as a hobo from time to time. He spent three years in the Army but I don't know what his duties were.

Mom was born in September 1923, also in Arkansas and spent most of her life here, too. As far as I know, she never "rode the rails" as a hobo, so it's quite probable that she never left the state until she got married and started a family.

Their two oldest kids were twin boys, born in August 1942. Etheal Ray and Cecil Ray. Cecil died when he was about 3 years and 6 months old. Next to come along was Shirley, in May 1945. I was the fourth child, born in October 1947. Steve Junior arrived in June 1951. After a gap of a few years, Robert was born in August 1957. Danny turned out to be the baby of the family, born in February 1960.

I'm ashamed to say that I don't know much about the early lives of my parents but it's obvious they had very rough lives. And to my great surprise, I just realized that Mom was only 18 when she gave birth to her first two sons. Why have I never considered that, before? Okay, maybe I shouldn't be so surprised at myself. After all, during most of my life, everything has been all about ME. Yeah, I know, maybe I really am just a jerk.

But I can say, with very little fear of contradiction, that I was probably one of the toughest men in Pope County. My feats, exploits and accomplishments as a farm laborer, as a close combat instructor (karate), as a Marine Corps Platoon Sergeant and later as a Platoon Commander are all sufficient proof of my strength, abilities and tenacity. But I was tough without being mean. I was strong without being a bully (in fact, when I was a teenager, the school bullies were afraid to pick on weaker students while I was anywhere around because I would not hesitate to "correct" their behavior).

I was also very strong, mentally. Peer pressure meant nothing to me. I never tried to gain popularity by going along with the crowd. I was very much my own man. I never smoked, drank or used drugs. Such things held no appeal for me. People used to say to me, "Don't knock it if you haven't tried it" but my reply would be, "Well, I have never been run over by a truck, either, but I don't have to try it to know that it could hurt me".

I truly do march to the beat of a different drummer. I freely admit that I have always been egotistical and stubborn but I earned the right to be that way.

Anyway, I'm writing this book to present my collection of remembrances that might hopefully entertain and enlighten you regarding the joys, pleasures, trials and tribulations of being a charter member of the Morris family.

Chapter 2

Day By Day

Although we traveled from time to time, following the crops or otherwise going where jobs were available, we generally lived in the Pope County area of Arkansas during most of my childhood years.

As a farm laborer, Dad cleaned out chicken houses and barns, using scoop shovels to load the chicken litter into old pickup trucks or mule drawn wagons and then used those shovels to spread the litter across pastures and crop areas. He tended livestock and poultry, built fences, cleared fence rows, worked at sawmills, hoed corn, hoed and picked cotton, and performed all sorts of manual labor. Especially, he hauled hay. Not just tons of hay but thousands of tons of hay. During my earliest years of working with him, we hauled loose hay, working with pitchforks to pile the hay on a flatbed wagon pulled by a team of mules. Often, the loose hay was used to make haystacks in areas where the cows could get to it in the wintertime. Other times, it was piled into haylofts or sheds, from which it could be pitched into mangers or feed lot areas. But mostly, the hay was hauled in the form of bales. These bales were generally 2 feet by 3 feet by 4 feet, fastened by two strands of either wire or twine. A bale could weigh anywhere from 60 to 90 pounds. These bales were stacked onto flatbed mule drawn wagons or pickup trucks for transport to barns or sheds, where they would be stacked "in the dry" and saved for winter feeding of the livestock.

That's how Dad provided for his family. He lived a harsh life and worked hard for every dollar that came into his possession. When he hauled hay, he was generally paid five cents per bale. When he worked by the hour, he earned 60 cents per hour.

When I describe how Dad provided for the family, I want you to understand that all of us kids played some very important roles in helping with our own upbringing. We all started working at very early ages. For example, our father would not have cleaned out as many chicken houses or hauled so much hay if we hadn't been right out there with him, shoveling manure and loading hay. Dad always said E. Ray was the only man alive who could load more hay than he could and still go out and have fun on a date after work.

There really wasn't a whole lot of competition for the job of cleaning out chicken houses but the Morris family was the best, no question about it. We generally had about a dozen different farmers all over Pope County for whom we performed this particular job, on a rotating basis, year round, and some of those farmers had more than one chicken house. Broiler chickens were kept only about 8 or 9 weeks per batch, in those days, so we stayed busy. We worked hard and fast, so there were very few occasions when we could not fit the next available job into our schedule. There was one particular farmer who thought he could get a better deal than we were giving him and hired three men to clean his houses rather than letting us do it. We worked for 60 cents per hour per man and he hired these guys at 50 cents per hour per man. He thought he was getting a better deal and he didn't tell us he didn't need us until we went over there to do the work. Dad was mad. We had been counting on that work. As it turns out, that farmer drove 6 miles to the Atkins "bottoms" to pick up these guys every morning and drove them home at night. They took two days longer to do the job than we usually took and he wound up feeding them lunch each day. He really lost money on that deal--and we never worked for him again. That's the only time I ever knew Dad to hold a grudge.

I worked at my first job (outside the family) when I was 6 years old. I followed an old farmer who was plowing with a team of mules. Whenever he turned up a large root or a rock, I carried it to the edge of the field and threw it into the border or into a creek. Some of those roots and rocks were about as big as I was. The work day ran from daylight until dark and the pay was a quarter a day. But in those days, a quarter was big money. By the time I was 7, I was using a pitchfork to help haul loose hay or shoveling manure. Before I turned 12, I was earning a man's wage, working at sawmills and on farms, either alone or with Dad. For a long time, we worked for 60 cents an hour and I distinctly recall being amazed to know that every time a minute had passed, I had earned a penny. But I had to really work hard. Dad insisted that we give an honest hour's work for an honest hour's pay. And that's just my personal example of how all of us kids got into the business of helping to put beans and 'taters on the table. It was a source of great pride to know that we were sharing the responsibility, pulling our own weight, so to speak.

Along the way, I acquired a peculiar set of job skills. Skills that would not even be recognized as such, these days. For example, when I threw a bale of hay on the truck or trailer, I could throw it in such a way that it would land just about where it needed to be in the stack. Sometimes, a small nudge might be needed to get it seated properly, but hardly ever. Because of that skill, I could load most of the truck from the ground, which saved a lot of time by not having to climb onto the truck to place the bales from the bed of the truck. This was a particularly valuable skill since I generally hauled hay by myself. I had a 1950 model ford truck with a hay frame on it. That means the factory bed that came with the truck had been removed and replaced with a flat platform that provided a wider, longer base on which hay bales could be stacked. The truck had a 4-speed manual transmission with a floor shift. During most of the summer, the driver's door was removed. I could stick it in first gear and let it crawl across the hayfield by itself while I loaded hay from both sides of the truck.

All I had to do was reach in occasionally, to steer the truck. And I always worked at a run. As long as hay bales were available, I could load and stack 53 bales onto the truck in less than 15 minutes.

Another old-timey skill I acquired was driving a team of mules and a wagon. With a good team, I could back a wagon all the way through a 400 foot chicken house. You see, we would go all the way to the end of the chicken house with an empty wagon to start cleaning it out. As we shoveled manure into the wagon, we would pull forward a little at a time until the wagon was loaded. Then we could go straight out with the load to spread the manure over a pasture. Most chicken houses had a set of doors at only one end and it would have been too hard on the team to pull in and then try to back out with a loaded wagon. As time went by, I also got very good at backing a wagon through a chicken house with a tractor after working with horses and mules became a thing of the past.

Even shoveling manure was an acquired skill. In those days, chicken houses were usually cleaned to the ground after each set of broiler chickens and we used large scoop shovels to pick up and load the manure. When I threw a shovelful of manure on the wagon, I threw it in such a way that it stayed together, en masse, until it landed where I had aimed it. This took a certain flick of the wrist, which many people simply never mastered. Unloading the manure was not as easy as you might think, either If the bed of the wagon or truck was not smooth, I knew how to scrape up a shovelful of manure without damaging the face of the scoop by jamming it against a nail head or a bolt.

And of course, there was the skill of milking cows by hand. There were very few times when we actually had a cow of our own to milk. I don't think we ever really owned a cow, at all, but there were periods when we lived on a farm or worked for a farmer who allowed us to milk one of his cows. Also, one of our neighbors, Durard Burnett, was a dairy farmer and I did a lot of dairy-type work for him. There's nothing like milking cows to strengthen your wrists. Even up into my mid-40's, I could still break an apple in half with my bare hands. But milking cows is another one of those yesteryear skills that wouldn't have much application in today's job markets.

So, you see, there are some skills that you simply can't put on a resume and a lot of my abilities, in which I took considerable pride at the time, would have no meaning and no value in this day and age. Time marches on, sad to say. Sometimes, I have been able to successfully assimilate new required skills and sometimes I haven't. For example, my extensive experience with tractors and farm equipment gave me a natural ability to drive all kinds of forklifts in future jobs working in warehouses and industrial areas.

Anyway, we were a bunch of very competitive kids. We have all always loved a good challenge. Our lifestyle seemed good for our health, too. Farm labor kept us in pretty good shape. Being a girl didn't hold Shirley back, either. She has thrown more hay bales and shoveled more manure than most GUYS her age. Shirley and E. Ray spent a lot more time in the cotton fields than any of the rest of us kids, mostly because they started hoeing and picking cotton in the 1940's, while the rest of us didn't get started until just before the farmers started using those cotton picking machines and put us all out of a job, at least in that particular field of endeavor.

But Shirley and E. Ray were both experts at hoeing cotton and corn and I reckon either one of them could beat just about anybody at picking cotton. It takes a special kind of strength to go out to the fields at first light (that's a long time before actual sunup, by the way) and stay out there all day long, walking up and down a field, hoeing the weeds out of row after row of cotton or corn, until it got plumb too dark to see. Same thing with picking cotton. They would routinely spend 12 or 13 hours a day, walking through those cotton fields, dragging a cotton sack behind them. Those cotton sacks were probably ten or twelve feet long and had a strap that would fit over one shoulder so that you could stuff the cotton into the opening of the sack. That was backbreaking work because we stayed bent over almost all the time, leaning down to pick the cotton and hardly ever standing up straight even when we would stuff the handfuls of cotton into the sack.

I don't remember all the prices we got for picking cotton but by the time I got fully into the cotton picking business, we sometimes got up to three dollars per hundred pounds. Since they started at it long before I did, Shirley and E. Ray (not to mention our parents) had to work for less.

I know there are a lot of strong, tough people out there. People who could whip me without even raising a sweat. But I doubt if any of those so-called strong men could have stayed up with me in the hay field, or shoveling manure or stringing barbed wire. They would burn out fast. That's the difference between show-muscles and work-muscles.

Chapter 3

Entertainment

Part of our entertainment from outside sources was (sometimes) provided by a huge old battery powered radio. Those old radios might stand 3 or 4 feet tall and usually got only one or two stations (of course, they were strictly AM stations--there wasn't much FM traffic back in those days). The use of the radio was strictly controlled by the parents because the battery would run down after a couple of hours.

But most of our entertainment was strictly of the homemade variety. We kids played tag and hide-and-seek. Sometimes, we would get a bunch of old automobile or bicycle tires and roll them along the roads, trying to see how far and how fast we could push them while trying to keep them from falling over and trying to keep up with them on the downhill grades. We ran barefooted on dirt roads and thought nothing about it.

E. Ray might put us smaller kids inside an old tractor or truck tire and roll us along. All of us have gone down many a hill inside a tire. Yes, Shirley, too. We would even go down a hill with a creek at the bottom. Hitting the water was exciting. This was real fun.

Of course, y'all realize you could only do that sort of thing back in the good old days. Nowadays, if a Big Brother tried to put his little brothers and sisters into tires and roll them down a hill into a creek, then Big Brother would spend the rest of his life either behind bars for child abuse or in a rubber room under intense psychological evaluation.

But the most fun of all during the summer was going swimming. Our favorite spot was a swimming hole on Isabell Creek. Another good spot was Point Remove Creek at the low water bridge. In those days, people could actually swim in creeks and streams without worrying about pollution or toxic waste. We would go to the swimming hole in one of those old-timey cars, the kind with running boards and fenders. Really, it is not correct to say that we went "in" the car because most of us rode on the outside, standing on the running boards while hanging onto the door posts or straddling the fenders while hanging onto the hood ornament. Nobody wanted to ride on the back of the car because the dust would boil up pretty bad back there but, otherwise, there were usually a bunch of kids hanging all over the car. E. Ray usually got stuck doing the driving because he was Big Brother. That was only one of the many sacrifices he made for us. He was stuck inside the hot car while we all enjoyed ourselves. Come to think of it, he hardly ever even got a cool breeze because there was usually a kid standing on the running board right by the driver's door, hanging onto the outside mirror. Of course, back then, there were no seat belt laws. Plus, there were no seat belts. But again, if a Big Brother should drive around with kids hanging on outside the car in this day and age, it would be back to jail (or the rubber room) for Big Brother.

Another source of entertainment, winter or summer, was riding to town in a wagon drawn by a team of horses or mules. Our family generally always walked everywhere we went but there were a couple of periods of time when we were affluent enough to own a wagon and a couple of mules. Or maybe we just worked for a farmer who allowed us to use his equipment. Anyway, we loved riding that wagon. I recall sitting at the back of the wagon, dragging the end of a stick on the ground, making designs on the dirt road. Jumping off and climbing back on while the wagon was moving was a lot of fun, too. Sometimes, we played Cowboys and Indians. Excuse me, to be politically correct, I should say Bovine Boys and Native Americans but we have a little bit of Cherokee in our blood, so we played both sides. Anyway, with the help of legendary westerners like Roy Rogers and Gene Autry, we withstood many attacks and shot a lot of imaginary stagecoach robbers and highwaymen from behind the high sideboards of that wagon.

As we kids got older, another source of outside entertainment was the drive-in movie. Everybody would pile into an old car and we all would go to the picture show on dollar night. That's when a whole carload could get in for a dollar. Of course, after we got there, most of us would sit in chairs outside the car--or in front of the concession stand.

During the winter, we would mostly stay inside and play games at the kitchen table by the light of a kerosene lamp. Games like bingo, monopoly, checkers, dominoes or card games. The game of checkers was basically just a two-person game but all us kids could get involved in a game of dominoes---and the whole family might play a few hands of bingo. When we played checkers, we didn't always have actual checkers but we used soda pop bottle caps that we had picked up on the streets in town. One player would keep his bottle caps turned upside down to indicate either red or black. For some reason, jacks was considered a girls' game but I played that a lot, anyway. I didn't know the term manual dexterity back then but I enjoyed testing my hand speed trying to pick up all those jacks and catching that ball on the first bounce. And of course, we all played marbles, winter or summer. E. Ray was generally recognized as a local champion, although it was very rare that he ever played for keeps. That just wasn't his style. Those games would keep us entertained for hours when the cold winter wind would blow the snow and rain all around the house. Ah, the good old days.

Chapter 4

Special Treats

I have a very pleasant summer memory about when we were living near the foot of Crow Mountain in Atkins. I don't think it was IN Atkins at the time because the city limits didn't go out very far. Anyway, early on a Saturday morning, there was an old man who would come driving down off the mountain with a team of mules and a wagon. He would be headed for town with a load of watermelons and cantaloupes for sale. That wagon would be full of the most beautiful ripe vegetables, covered with hay. Produce fresh from the good earth, grown without chemicals or any modern devices, harvested by the caring, weathered hand of a true American farmer.

That old man had great pride in the fruits of his labors and yet, he had the honest, open country style humility that made it clear that he gave credit to his Maker for the gifts he had received. I remember him as a soft-spoken, smiling man with a weather-beaten face. A gentle hand with his animals and a tolerant attitude toward us Morris kids who climbed all over the sides of his wagon to inspect his goods.

We felt really special, too, because we got first pick of what he had for sale (because we lived at the foot of the mountain between his farm and the town). Most Saturdays, Dad had a few coins to buy something because he would get paid at his sawmill job on Friday evening. If I recall correctly, the watermelons were priced from 35 to 50 cents and the cantaloupes were two for a quarter.

After a watermelon was purchased, it would be placed either in a creek or under the edge of the house out of the sun to wait for the feast to begin. By mid-afternoon, the anticipation was almost too much to bear. We never ate the watermelons in the house, always outside. For us kids, it was your basic picnic but for the adults, it was a way to keep from adding an extra million flies inside the house.

Another favorite visitor was the iceman. When we lived way out in the country, he would come by once or twice a week. He drove an ancient truck. Yes, even for those days, this vehicle was already a relic. I can't swear to it but I think the price of a 25-lb block of ice was a quarter. Of course, we couldn't afford ice every week but when we could, it was wonderful.

During the summertime, a small chunk of ice was our replacement for a candy bar. We kept the block of ice in a galvanized metal washtub covered with a quilt. I never did quite figure out why that didn't make the ice melt a lot faster. The quilt would stick to the ice where it touched. I didn't understand that, either. Well, okay, the truth is I'm pushing 66 and I still haven't figured out any of that stuff. Sometimes, we would see how long we could stand to have our hand against the ice. At least once, I tried to see how long I could sit on the ice with just the quilt and my britches between me and the ice. I could sit there long enough that my trousers would get wet, the quilt would stick to the ice and I would leave the impression of my tushy on top of the ice. It was a real treat to run around on a hot summer afternoon with a tiny sliver of ice clutched in our hands so we could bite off a tiny chunk every once in a while or just feel the coldness of it running through our fingers.

Another special memory I have of my early youth is having a bottle of soda pop with supper. We were living on the outskirts of Russellville. I don't remember where Dad was working, at the time but about every three weeks or so, he would send E. Ray to a store to buy a few soda pops. Sometimes, I would get to go along, even though it made the trip take longer because I couldn't walk as fast as E. Ray. Anyway, for supper, there might be pinto beans, mashed 'taters and biscuits. Occasionally, there might also be a bit of sausage as a side dish, although any kind of meat was a rarity in those days. But each child would get his (or her) own personal soda pop, not to be shared with anybody. We would each pour the soda pop into a glass over some precious chipped ice. That made the soda pop last longer. And the soda bottle would sit on the table near our plates so we'd know how much was left. That way, we could pace our eating and drinking to have a couple of healthy swigs left after we had cleaned our plates. Sodas were a nickel, then. There was also a two cent deposit on each bottle but you would get that back, in cash, when you returned the bottle to the store.

I know it sounds strange, now-a-days, to be speaking of a slice of watermelon, a chunk of ice or an occasional soda pop as being such highly memorable treats but we learned to have a sincere appreciation for whatever we got. I'm not saying we should take anything away from today's kids but maybe we could dole it out at a slightly less rapid pace to make their special treats and gadgets a little less commonplace. Then they might have more appreciation for what they have.

Thicker Than Water

Roy Morris

Notable Characters

Chapter 5

E. Ray

There must be something magical and mysterious about Firstborns. They seem to have powers and abilities far beyond the rest of us. I have been acquainted with one of these special people my entire life and he never ceases to amaze me. He is my brother. He was born on August 16th, 1942. By normal standards, he would be considered quite old, except for one thing…he can't be judged by normal standards. He is a Firstborn.

In fact, he was half of a set of identical twins. His twin, Cecil Ray, died at the age of three years and six months. Since that time, E. Ray has been "living for two" to make up for the life that was lost. And his life has certainly been full enough for two. He has a list of accomplishments which makes the achievements of others pale in comparison.

He didn't get the chance to formally graduate from high school because he had to go to work helping Dad provide for the family so he finished his education while he was in the Army. He has always believed that when one door closes, another door opens.

He was a very handsome young man. I'm no judge of good looking males because I have always concentrated on good looking females, instead, but E. Ray could easily have worked in the movies as a double for the young Elvis Presley.

He is as comfortable with a double-bladed ax or a sledge hammer as he is with a chain saw. He can drive a motorcycle, a dump truck or a bulldozer. In his youth, he did a lot of work with a pair of mules but he is equally talented with any piece of farm equipment.

He started earning a man's wage before he entered his teens because he did a man's share of the work, hauling hay, cleaning out chicken houses and barns and doing every type of farm work.

He is a wonder to watch when involved in a project requiring patience, ingenuity and skill. For example, when I brought several paintings home from Japan, he built frames for them that rival any that could have been purchased from a professional woodworker.

He completely remodeled his own home, converted a two-car garage into a very nice apartment and built another house on the back edge of his property.

Just like the boy scouts, he is "always prepared" because he does his homework for any task which he has set for himself. When he did the work on his house and those two other buildings, his structural designs, wiring, plumbing and carpentry work were good enough to pass certification inspections.

He has tremendous drive and focuses that drive precisely on the task or problem at hand. He solves those problems and completes those tasks because of his ability to focus, to apply himself in such a manner that a successful completion is a foregone conclusion. Failure is simply not an option.

He is an excellent golfer, a demon on the tennis courts, a formidable opponent in a bowling alley and a terror on a pool table or snooker table. He only weighs about 160 pounds and doesn't carry any fat but neither does he have the rippling muscles of a body builder. However, he has a tremendous amount of tendon strength and incredible energy. His hands and arms aren't huge but you would not want to challenge him at arm wrestling or have a gripping contest with him. You would lose.

When he was 50, he could run a six minute mile over a 3-mile course and he was able to run a seven minute mile over a 10-mile course. He regularly took part in races and marathons ranging from 3 miles on up to 26 miles per event. He routinely ran up Mount Nebo (near Dardanelle, Ark). He qualified for the Boston Marathon more than once.

He may have missed his calling as an athletic trainer. He could run any course at any pace with another person. Afterward, he could critique and analyze that person's running ability and set up a personal training regimen suited to that person's talents. Then, he could predict when that person would be able to run a given distance in a specified time. He did this by not only taking into account that person's height, weight, breath control and running style, but also by gauging that person's character and initiative.

When he competed, he did occasionally get beaten, but only by the best, and even they had to set personal records to stay ahead of him because he would compete with all of his energy right up to the finish line. As he always said, "It ain't over 'till it's over". However, he was most certainly not just a runner. He would snow ski on the most challenging slopes when he would vacation in Colorado. And he would extend his balancing act to the many lakes and watersheds at home in Arkansas, where he would water ski and slalom like a pro.

But, for all his athletic abilities and physical powers, he does not concentrate on that aspect of his life. He is a deacon in his church and his faith in God is rock-solid. He never tries to push his religious ideals on anybody but he never fails to credit his Maker with all the good things that have been part of his life and is never shaken by any minor problems or difficulties. He accepts each individual at face value with no prejudice.

E. Ray is a very complex individual. He has written many articles and short stories covering a wide variety of subjects. In fact, he wrote a book entitled *Odd Lot Collection.*

Many people don't have time in their lives to even read a book, much less write one. I attribute this to his unique concept of time. He never wastes it. He has the same 24 hours in a day as everyone else but he uses time so efficiently and effectively that he seem to be living in a time warp of some kind.

He does everything in a very neat manner. He is not fastidious but he does think there is a place for everything and everything should be in its place. However, he doesn't take it to extreme. For many years, he drove a very old, rather beat-up truck. He kept it clean but he didn't pamper it. When he hauled a load of wood, he loaded it until the bumper dragged the ground. That old truck was ugly to some people but it was kept in excellent running condition. Whenever he was asked why he didn't put fancy wheels on it or fix it up, he would simply say, "If it ain't broke, don't fix it". At the same time, however, he keeps his wife's car immaculate and mechanically perfect.

He retired from the Firestone plant in Russellville, Arkansas after more than 30 years of working at a job that he didn't particularly enjoy because he says, "Variety is the spice of life, but monotony pays the bills". But I might add that he was always highly respected for the high quality of the work he did at the plant.

He's a good family man. His marriage to his wife, Jannie, has been solid since their wedding in 1961. They share love, mutual understanding and respect for each other and their relationship is genuine, strong and eternal. She calls him "Honey" and he refers to her as "The Boss".

He gave me a place to live, money to live on and the use of his truck after I lost my job, my wife and my self-respect. He gave me the strength to survive and pick up the pieces of my life after the death of my daughter. He helped me find, not one, but several jobs until I settled in with one that suited me. When the time came for me to leave Arkansas to accept a job in North Carolina, he helped me buy a truck, covered my travel expenses and gave me enough money to live on until I would start drawing a paycheck.

E. Ray went through some tough times during Dad's extended period of failing health and hospital stays during the last years of his life. On many occasions, E. Ray stretched his financial situation to the limit. He did this very quietly, with no fanfare and without asking for help. His strong sense of responsibility as Firstborn was his only guide, his only motivation for the actions he took in response to the requirements placed on him.

E. Ray had to put Dad into the hospital…sometimes when Dad didn't want to go. He was troubled by the fact that he had placed himself, or had been forced into, a position of authority over Dad's freedom but he did what he had to do, for Dad's benefit.

E. Ray took the brunt of Dad's anger, even though he had no choice but to take sides with the doctors against Dad's wishes to be left alone. There is no way anybody but a Firstborn could have possessed the strength, the will or the love to make all the decisions E. Ray had to make regarding Dad's welfare.

One of his decisions…the most burdensome, most frightening and most difficult was one which he had made years ago. You see, the doctors knew when Dad was reaching the end of his strength, the end of his ability to withstand the pain, the end of his will to live. Shirley and Steve Junior were at the hospital at the time. Shirley called E. Ray to let him know the time had come and to ask if he wanted Dad put on artificial life support. E. Ray had the courage, the strength and the faith in God to say, "No, use no heroic measures".

This type of thing is something he and I had discussed from time to time. He has a deep respect for life but he believes it should be a complete life. A type of life that would result from being dependent on machines to breathe for you or to keep your heart beating would be only a half-life…and that would be worse than no life, at all. Both of us had decided that we would request "no heroic measures" to avoid such an existence.

But when the time came to give that answer for Dad, I'm glad I didn't have to do it.

I cannot estimate, and nobody will ever know, the pressure and the self-doubts that E. Ray endured since he told the doctors to allow Dad to die naturally, if it was inevitable. He asked only that Dad be kept comfortable, with as little pain as possible.

I had visited with Dad for a few days at the time of his birthday when he turned 69. He was in the hospital at that time. After that, E. Ray and Shirley had kept me informed of Dad's condition by phone. When I was told it was time to come home, I knew it would be to see Dad for the last time. As it turned out, Dad actually died before I got on the road. The family decided not to call me back to let me know because they didn't want his death to be weighing on my mind while I drove over a thousand miles.

E. Ray made the funeral arrangements. He took care of all the details at the hospital. He arranged for a minister. He even cleaned out Dad's apartment and took care of his final bills.

But that wasn't the last of it, by any means. He took me to the funeral parlor to see Dad. He didn't tell me where we were going until we were almost there. He didn't want our destination to be bothering me. He also took Shirley to the funeral parlor for her first viewing of Dad in the casket. This had hit her very hard and I'm glad she had him for the support that only he could give.

After the funeral, E. Ray took me for a drive around the countryside and showed me the place where I had been born and told me a lot of family stories that I had forgotten.

During his entire life, E. Ray has been a tower of strength, a shining example for his fellow men, a leader by any standard and my personal idol. I know a lot more about this man that I simply have no way of expressing in a way that could be understood. I don't intend to imply that he was "bigger than life". He's a human being with human frailties and he has surely made his share of mistakes but he seems to bounce back from his own mistakes and from the other misfortunes that life will throw at a person, and he has done so with dignity, grace and optimism.

I have benefited greatly from my association with him. I am proud to call "Brother" this very extraordinary man who is living life to the fullest, this unstoppable, unbeatable uncommon "common man" who upholds the finest ideals of honor, courage and integrity. This man is Firstborn.

Chapter 6

Shirley Ann

Shirley is a Firstborn, too, in her own unique way. She is the first (and only) girl born in our family. Truly, she is one of a kind. To say that the Angels made her and then broke the mold would be a gross understatement. If we consider only her gender, you might say it was one girl against ALL us boys and she definitely had us outnumbered.

After shoveling manure or working in the hayfield or cotton field with us all day, she would get home and help Mom take care of the young'uns, do housework and prepare supper. In those days, it never occurred to me how terribly unfair that was. But I have mentioned already how self-centered I was as a kid, how life was all about me. And I might as well confess that I haven't changed much.

Anyway, Shirley was a regular little dynamo when she was a kid. And I can assure you, the aging process hasn't slowed her down, at all. And she is SO beautiful, you would not believe she could truly be related to any of us ugly boys--plus, if you saw us all together, you would easily believe she's the youngest of the bunch.

She is beyond smart and she is super-talented. For just a few examples, consider these items of information. She taught herself how to play a guitar and has been a member of several bluegrass and gospel bands, over the years. She was also partly responsible for bringing Arkansas its first Bluegrass Festival on Petit Jean Mountain.

Shirley sings with the voice of an Angel. She was nominated as Female Vocalist of the Year (Traditional) by the Arkansas Bluegrass

Association. She even passed on her musical abilities to her children and grandchildren. Both of her daughters, Jo and Gini, are really good singers and her son, Jason, was nominated as Male Vocalist of the Year (Contemporary) AND as Bluegrass Mandolin of the Year by the Arkansas Bluegrass Association. At one particular performance which I attended with two of our brothers, Robert and Dan, we were given a very special treat. Well, anytime we get to hear her pick and sing is a special treat but on this occasion, as I recall, she was accompanied on stage by her husband Dennis, son Jason, daughters Jo and Gini, and granddaughters Lacey Cheyenne and Savana Grace. The talent on that stage could have filled the auditorium at the Grand Old Opry. I might also mention that another granddaughter, Jessie, performed with a professional troupe as an interpretive dancer.

She sings the old-timey gospel and bluegrass songs. How she is able to remember the words and music to all those songs is a mystery to me. But she also writes her own songs (both words and music) and has produced several music cd's.

Her talents and abilities aren't just musical in nature, however. She got started in the newspaper business as a community correspondent and copy editor for the Petit Jean Country *Headlight* newspaper in Perry County and eventually served as editor, reporter and photographer.

She served as clerk of the Perry County Municipal Court for many years and was a part-time substitute teacher at Perryville High School. She served as vice president of the Perryville PTA and as county publicity chairman for the American Cancer Society (for which she received an award). She also served as recorder for the city of Adona and as treasurer for the Adona PTA.

She was a member of the nominating committee for the county Farm Family of the Year and was on the advisory committee of the Perry County Fair Association. She served as chairman of the entertainment program for the Perry County Fair. She was recognized by the Perryville Boy Scouts for her efforts in publicity provided for the troop.

This is just a brief synopsis and I don't even know everything she has done because I was gone for many years, in the Marines and working in other states, but I can tell you that, because of her numerous accomplishments, she was included in *Who's Who of American Women*

I may as well mention that she works as well with her hands as with her mind. She is very talented at painting, gardening, landscaping, interior decoration, arts and crafts. She helped Dennis build their home and I assure you, it is beautiful--a real showplace. I just don't think there is anything she can't do. She even gets together with our sister-in-law, Jannie, to assist with one of Jannie's MANY talents---making flower arrangements when it's time to decorate the local cemeteries.

All things considered, she hasn't turned out bad for a kid who started out as a 95-lb girl pulling a 100-lb cotton sack across a hot, dusty cotton field.

Chapter 7

Steve Junior

He's the next Morris kid behind me so we hung out together a lot. He has a lot more capabilities than I have. And I think he might be the only boy of the family who can sing. I have never heard him sing but I have heard reports about it. I didn't hear of anybody throwing fruit and vegetables at him to get him to shut up and Shirley hasn't disowned him, so I guess he has a reasonable voice. I can't recall that I ever heard E. Ray sing, either. That doesn't mean he never tried but I haven't heard any reports about it, one way or the other, so that could go either way. However, I HAVE heard Robert and Danny sing and I can absolutely assure you--they can't sing any better than I can. In fact, they are the only two people on earth who keep me from being the worst singer in the world.

Another talent Junior has that I don't have is mechanical ability. If a vehicle won't run, he can make it run. Doesn't matter what might be wrong with it. He can figure out what the problem is--and then figure out what to do about it. He can take a car apart and put it back together again…and it will actually run. If I took a vehicle apart, I would have to sell the pieces as scrap metal.

Electrical work, plumbing, telephone line repair, carpentry. It doesn't matter. He has a talent for all of these things. And he's another Morris kid who built his own house, just like E. Ray and Shirley. What happened? Why did all of these skills and abilities come out so naturally in both of them and then skip right over me to land on Steve Junior?

When Junior joined the Army, he went Airborne, of course. There he was, jumping out of perfectly good airplanes. Oh, sure, he had a parachute but all you need is for just ONE of those things to fail to work and that's the end of that story. Okay, actually, while I was in the Marine Corps on Okinawa, I attended a parachute training school which was administered by the Army Special Forces unit (Green Berets) at Fort Buckner, but I got shipped off from there to Viet-Nam to fill a quota in an Engineer Battalion before I took my qualifying jump, so my insanity was only temporary.

But Junior was always jumping out of or off of everything he could climb up on. When he was a kid, he would play "Tarzan" by jumping off of bluffs and grabbing tree limbs on the way down. I think I pushed him off the end of the porch in his stroller just one time too many when I was babysitting for him. Maybe it's all my fault.

And he's tough. Double tough. If' there is one man in Arkansas who might have been able to haul more hay or shovel more manure than I could, he would be that man. He can withstand cold weather a lot better than I can, too. I've had a lot of injuries to my arms and legs so I have poor circulation in my limbs but being able to work in the cold isn't always a question of survival by wearing enough layers. Sometimes, it's just a matter of mental toughness, and he has more of that than I have.

Chapter 8

Robert Lee

Robert is 10 years younger than I am, so I never got to interact with him very much as a kid. And he grew up in a different world than I did, in a manner of speaking. By the time he was six or seven years old, the family was generally living in houses that usually had electricity, if not running water, so he doesn't have memories of walking to town with the entire family or riding in horse-drawn wagons. By the time he got old enough to start thinking about driving cars, running boards were pretty much a thing of the past.

Not to say that he had it any easier than I did, by any stretch. Sure, Dad was earning a little more money per hour but the price of everything had also gone way up (and at a much faster rate than the minimum wage) so the family was still always far behind the financial power curve.

Robert was only 9 years old when I left home to join the Marines, so we didn't relate to each other during his teen years and, even later on, I would be home for only a week or two at a time while on vacation, so we didn't have much impact on each other's lifestyle.

I do know we definitely have different tastes in music. He has always liked the hard rock group *Kiss* but I have never been able to understand a word they were singing and as near as I could tell, their music didn't sound like music--it just sounded like noise. I guess it must be an acquired taste. He likes hard rock, like *Hootie and The Blowfish, ZZ Top, Def Leppard,* and *Bon Jovi* while I never strayed away from *The Beach Boys, Jan and Dean, The Four Seasons, Ricky Nelson, Motown* and old-time country music.

He worked for many years at the Atkins Public School. At a very early age, he took on the responsibility of looking after Mom because all of us older kids were married off and gone. He did this with no fanfare, no comments and no complaints and he continued to do this for many years.

These days, he works as a maintenance man at an apartment complex where he lives. The two of us get together with Dan from time to time, just to shoot a little pool or maybe go up to visit with Shirley and Dennis, mostly on special occasions or holidays.

Chapter 9

Danny Ray

Danny is more than 13 years younger than I am, so we basically never really interacted as kids, at all. I know practically nothing about his life during his teen years because, as with Robert, I saw him for only a week or two at a time when I was home on vacation or a couple of times when the family came to wherever I was stationed to visit with me and my wife, Juanita.

He got into the martial arts and progressed steadily up through the ranks but during October 1996, he had a slight mishap. You see, he is a Black Belt Tae Kwon Do Instructor, licensed and certified as such by not only the United States Tae Kwon Do Federation, but also by the International Tae Kwon Do Federation. The problem is, he doesn't LOOK like a Black Belt. He appears to be just an ordinary human being. He's not a towering hulk with a steely-eyed stare. So, there is occasionally some idiot who wants to make an instant reputation for himself by beating Dan in a "fair" fight. Sort of like in the Old West, when the local no-name punk tried to take on a real-life gunslinger.

Dan was in Morrilton when a guy tried this method of acquiring quick fame but he got only cracked ribs and a concussion for his efforts. He slashed Dan across the back with a knife while Dan was getting into his truck. Dan whirled, kicked him in the sternum, then elbowed him in the back of the neck as he doubled over.

Of course, Dan was temporarily suspended by the USTF and the ITF. This was not done as a punitive measure but simply because it is standard procedure following such an incident pending investigation. Dan was cleared and reinstated. Dan doesn't start fights. He finishes them. Each time an opponent says, "I'm going to kick your butt", Dan replies, "You won't be the first one to try but you can be the next one to fail.

The first thing a student learns is the Tae Kwon Do Creed, which stresses restraint, dignity and respect for others. Tae Kwon Do Masters are actually pacifists. However, if you should fail to recognize and respect their pacifism, they have the ability to "pacify" you to the point where you WILL respect it. And I can verify that Dan is fast. Extremely fast. I have sparred with him on several occasions and the only reason I landed any blows at all is because I am the Big Brother. Mind you, now, this is not to say that his Tae Kwon Do is superior to my Shorin-Ryu Karate. I was active in my style during the late '60s, '70s and '80s while he was most active during the late '80s, '90s and beyond.

But that whole incident was sort of funny, considering Mom's reaction when she saw the condition of Dan's clothes and his back after he was slashed. She was only about 80 pounds, but I would have hated to be that slasher if she had got hold of him.

For many years, Dan has worked as a maintenance man at the Diamond International Truck repair/service shop in Russellville. He passed the test to get his CDL certificate--that means he can drive semi-trucks--and he occasionally shuttles a few big rigs around the state between various Diamond facilities.

After Robert got married off late in life, Dan took over the responsibility of taking care of Mom. As his brother had before him, he assumed this job with no complaints and no requests for assistance. As I mentioned in the previous chapter, I occasionally get together with him and Robert just to "hang".

Thicker Than Water

Roy Morris

The Daily Struggle

Chapter 10

Indian Head Nickel

I can't remember how old I was when this event occurred, although I believe I must have been somewhere around five years old. I was old enough to know that I should not want something if it meant others would have to make sacrifices to give me my heart's desire but I was still young enough to think I might get my way if I cried long and loud.

It was a very hot summer day. The family was in town. Going to town was a pretty rare event in those days but it was something we did as a family. We were walking, of course. During that period, we walked everywhere we went. It seemed to be the natural order of things.

I was tired beyond description but I was too old to be carried. Besides, I was not the youngest of the family as my brother, Steve Junior, was a mere "babe in arms". However, I was small enough to just sit down in the dirt and cry as if my heart was broken. You see, I wanted an ice cream. I wanted it more than anything else in the world. I NEEDED it. My continued existence on planet Earth depended on my obtaining it.

Asking, begging, demanding had all been to no avail. Crying inconsolably was my last resort--because we were about to walk past the last store on the way out of town. It was DO OR DIE for an Eskimo pie.

My older brother, E. Ray, had a nickel. He'd had it for quite a while. It was a rare and special nickel...one of those Indian Head (or

Buffalo) nickels. It was already very old, even at that time. Indian Head nickels were first minted in 1913, so that coin may have been already about forty years old.

All those facts were unknown to me. If I had known, I would not have understood. If I had understood, I might not have cared. Only two things were known to me. I knew I wanted an ice cream. And I knew that E. Ray had what it would take to get me one. Well, I got that ice cream. The memory of it lives on in my mind. The wonder of that sweet, cold, creamy, ever-so-delicious confectionary treat still weaves it pleasurable way through the strands of my memory. The smooth and wondrous taste of it still lingers on my tongue, even after all these years. I could go out right now and buy a whole gallon of ice cream and eat it all in one sitting, if I so desired. But a dozen gallons would not match the pure delight I got from that single ice cream on a stick.

I don't know why E. Ray gave up that treasured Indian Head nickel for something as fleeting as an ice cream bar (of which he did not get a single bite, by the way). Maybe he did it out of caring and understanding. Maybe he was ordered to, by our Dad. Maybe he just simply did it to shut up the crybaby. Do the reasons really matter, now? The bottom line is this: He did it.

During all our lives, I have been a taker and he has been a giver. If I counted up the value of all the articles he has given me, the personal time he has spent doing things with me or for me and the actual cash he has handed over to me....well, I would have to win the lottery to have any hope of ever breaking even with him. But of course, that's the same situation I have with my sister, Shirley. Two astonishingly large debts that will never be repaid.

Anyway, fast forward to 1995. I had come into possession of an American Frontier Nickel Set, consisting of six Indian Head nickels, encased in plastic so both sides of the coins were visible. They were minted in 1924, 1928, 1935, 1936 and 1937, respectively. Their value certainly could not compare to the coin that E. Ray gave up for me because we'll never know how much it might have been worth. But for his birthday in 1995, I gave him that set of coins.

I cannot duplicate the circumstances under which he made his gift, nor can I ever compensate him for the value of the many gifts he has given. I can only imitate the gesture of giving. I had the good fortune to be born into such an incredible family. The values we have placed on our kinship-our family ties-have been phenomenal. On those occasions when it seemed as if it was US against the whole World, we have never felt outnumbered because our common bond made us as strong as we needed to be.

I don't know what motivates the members of other families to hold together against all odds but for us, it has been the knowledge that blood is Thicker Than Water and although our debts to each other have been numerous and large, the bills have always been marked "Paid In Full".

Chapter 11

How Brave, the Young

Many tales of bravery describe acts of courage and selflessness performed in combat on the battlefield, in dark alleys during the still of the night or perhaps even on highways when accidents occur.

I would like to tell about two acts of unselfish bravery and uncommon gallantry which occurred in the mid 1950's in a small garden spot in a quiet, peaceful pasture in rural Arkansas on a bright and beautiful afternoon.

The two people involved may not even remember the incident but that does not lessen the importance of their actions and the passage of time has not diminished my admiration for these two people. I am speaking of my older brother, E. Ray and my sister, Shirley.

Our little clan, the Morris family, was exceedingly poor when we were living in a rented house near the intersection of highway 105 and 247. The house was owned by a country gentleman named Reese Alewine, who allowed us to live there in exchange for Dad's services as a farm laborer. Mister Alewine also permitted us to do a little bit of gardening in a section of one of his pastures.

The house was situated on top of a small hill with a beautiful view of the surrounding countryside. The back and one side of the hill were covered with trees, through which a path led to the bottomland where our humble garden was located not far from a creek.

On this particular afternoon, after we had changed from our school clothes into our work clothes, we walked down the path to do a little hoeing, groundbreaking and weed pulling in our garden. Shirley and E. Ray led the way and I lagged along behind, on the lookout for squirrels, rabbits and birds along the way. Mom was up at the house, tending our younger brother, Steve Junior and working on preparations for supper.

Unknown to us, there was a small herd of cows which had been temporarily put into the pasture to await loading for shipment to the sale barn at Atkins. They were mostly mild-mannered dairy cows but some of them were "muley" cows, half-wild critters which were almost impossible to catch if they ever got out of a pen or pasture and they were generally more trouble than they were worth. There were only about 25 cows in that herd but their unexpected presence would add an element of shock to the situation which was to occur.

While we were working in the garden, the herd had been grazing on the front side of the hill when they were spooked by something. Perhaps it was the surprise appearance of a dog or some other animal but, for some reason, the herd stamped and came running madly around the base of the hill, heading straight for our garden.....and us.

There was no fence around our garden spot and when we looked up from our work, the cows were only about 30 yards from us. I distinctly remember a feeling of pure terror that washed through me when I saw those hooves and horns coming toward us. However, while my fear resulted in my being frozen in place, the fear that E. Ray and Shirley must surely have felt had infinitely different results. Their reactions to the crisis were heroic and instantaneous. In the same split-second, E. Ray grabbed a big handful of weeds and charged directly toward that thundering herd, waving his arms and yelling like he was crazy while Shirley jumped in front of me, as if trying to protect me with her own body and she also started shouting and waving her arms. Luckily, the herd turned away from E. Ray, so Shirley's self-sacrifice was not required. The herd ran past us down toward the creek, where they eventually stopped of their own accord.

Would that herd have run over us? Since there was no fence, would they have turned away from us, anyway, even if E. Ray and Shirley had done nothing? I cannot say with certainty, but I suspect not because I starkly remember the look in their eyes. I believe we all would have suffered serious injury or even death, if not for the determination and bravery exhibited that day by my brother and sister. In my heart, I know that I owe my life to those two children, who were hero and heroine just as surely as any soldier who ever charged against an enemy and just as surely as any fire fighter who ever ran into a burning building to save someone.

As I said, the incident may not be a significant memory for either of my two idols but that does not affect me. I can only marvel at the nobility of character, the purity of heart, the love and the courage those two individuals must possess, to have performed such acts. I can only hope that, before I die, I may be able to do something to show them both how deeply they are loved and how highly they are esteemed by their little brother.

Chapter 12

Working While Sick

It was the winter of 1963. I had barely turned 16 and was the oldest child still living at home. Dad, Mom and my three younger brothers completed the family unit after E. Ray and Shirley had "married off". We were living in Oak Grove, Arkansas in a small board frame house owned by a man named Geno Johnston. Our rent, water and electricity were free because Dad was employed by Mr. Johnston to take care of two chicken houses that had been built the same time as the house. In fact, we had helped build everything. It was weird having electricity and indoor plumbing. Very nice but weird.

Anyway, these were no paltry chicken coops. Each house held thousands of laying hens. Every day, Dad and Mom fed and watered the chickens and gathered, inspected, washed, separated and packed thousands of eggs. It was a family operation. My brothers and I worked before and after school, and especially on weekends, to help our parents get the chores done. We repaired feed line chains, cleaned water troughs, changed the straw and pine shavings in the nests, inoculated chickens, whitewashed the roofs of the chicken houses and did a multitude of other chores aimed at keeping the place in operation. And we handled a LOT of eggs.

Well, the whole family caught the flu, all at the same time. My Dad was the toughest, hardest-working man I have ever known but the flu really hit him hard that winter. He pushed himself far past the point of exhaustion and, by the time he ran out of reserve energy, Mom and my brothers were already bedridden. They were all so sick.

I was sick, too. But I was the oldest child still living at home so I had a burden of responsibility resting squarely on my shoulders. Passing the buck had never been an option in our family, so I would not have tried to get out of my obligation, even if there had been anybody available to take over for me.

Luckily, I had been in excellent condition before the flu got to me. Not only did I have the natural vitality of a clean-living, athletic, teenaged country boy but I had also spent a great deal of time lifting weights, swimming, climbing mountains, running and doing gymnastics to supplement my usual activities, such as hauling hay, shoveling manure and doing various other outdoor farm jobs. I had the physical strength and endurance to do all the things that needed to be done. Furthermore, I had the mental toughness, the initiative and the determination to force my body to do all these things.

If there had ever been a young man who was totally prepared, in every possible way, to contend with a critical situation, I was that young man. In fact, if I had not been sick, I would not have realized that there was a crisis, in the first place. After all, nothing is ever impossible to the young.

The Morris family had a responsibility. Simple as that. If the entire family was able to work together to discharge that responsibility, that was all well and good. But if it was necessary for one given member of the family to be THE ONE who took care of business, that was all the same to us. I was that one, at that time. I cleaned, cooked, fed the family and kept that egg operation going. I was just doing what had to be done. I didn't feel martyred or unjustly used. All that I accomplished during that time, everything I did, it was just for the family. That was our way.

Sure, I had periods of weakness. Sometimes, I would feel so dizzy, I would have to sit down for a while to get my bearings. I felt sort of like a zombie. Many times, I walked over to the neighborhood store to pick up medicine or food and I made numerous trips between the house and the chicken houses and I would find myself suddenly AT some destination and I would have absolutely no memory of having made the trip. But I did not surrender to the sickness until the rest of the family was up and about.

This is only one of a long series of incidents and episodes that had a profound effect on my personality during my formative years. Anybody who knows me will probably tell you that I am the most stubborn human being that ever lived. And I am most certainly not a person of immaculate and sterling character but I do have a strong sense of commitment to family and I view each new position of responsibility or each new challenge as simply another opportunity to excel.

I'm a pretty lucky guy. My family has forgiven a multitude of sins, errors in judgment and dumb mistakes and I have turned to my family for help hundreds of times when there was simply no help to be had from any other quarter. And each time that I have had to seek forgiveness, beg for mercy or ask for assistance, positive family response has always been instantaneous and unconditional. For no other reason than that of common ancestry. When I have had no other redeeming qualities, I have always been able to rely on blood ties because blood is Thicker Than Water and a Morris will always do for the family.

Chapter 13

Extremely Stupid

Have you ever thought about how many times you did something extremely stupid when you were a youngster? During the summer of 1964, Steve Junior and I went to a movie with our two best friends, Lavon and Larry Johnston. No, going to the movie was not the stupid part--that came later.

The movie was the original black and white old-timey version of a movie called *The Hand* and was being shown at the old walk-in theater in Russellville. I don't recall the name of the theater but it was about a block down from the courthouse on the other side of the street. The four of us met some more friends, Ronnie and Fred Davis, outside the theater and we all decided to sit in the balcony. We all wound up in the front row of the balcony, looking right over the railing. Ronnie was in the last seat against the wall and I was in the first seat by the aisle.

Okay, now, back in those days (yes, those famous "good old days"), the movies were not really very gory. Most of the violence and horror were left up to the imagination of the viewer. But there was this one part where the hand was crawling across the back of the seat of a car while a guy was driving alone late at night. Then it leaped for his throat.

Keep that in mind while I tell you this. I had decided to scare Ronnie. It was really dark in there so I slid slowly out of my seat into the aisle. A couple of the guys next to me knew what I was doing but they went along with it. Still crouching, I moved back a couple of rows and crawled over until I was behind Ronnie.

My timing was perfect. Just as that hand jumped for that driver's throat in the movie, I leaned way down and grabbed Ronnie by the neck. There was a bloodcurdling scream and Ronnie headed for parts unknown. We caught him by the back of his shirt and one leg just before he jumped clean over the railing. Needless to say, we don't have any idea where his popcorn and soda landed.

Okay, that was pretty stupid, right? Wait, there's more. Lavon and Larry had ridden to the movie with Junior and me. We had an old 1956 Ford station wagon. Lavon drove, going home after the movie. Junior and I were sitting in the back seat, while Larry and Lavon were up front. I had set it up that way because I had another great plan. And I had not learned my lesson, yet.

The trip home was uneventful until we got through Atkins and had turned off of Hwy 105 onto Hwy 247, headed for our community of Economy. At the turn-off, we opened up the back of the station wagon. It was a warm night and we enjoyed the cool draft. And it was another part of my master plan.

There weren't anywhere near as many houses on Hwy 247 back then as there are now and it could be a pretty spooky road, especially after seeing such a great horror movie. Our conversations and imaginations were going wild.

After we crossed the twin Gum Log bridges, I crawled sneakily out of the back seat into the rear of the station wagon, out the back hatch, onto the roof and started making my way toward the front of the vehicle. Mind you, now, we were going about 40 mph.

Somewhere between the Travis place and the Murdoch place, I got to the front of the car, reached in through the driver's window and grabbed Lavon by the shoulder. I seem to recall another bloodcurdling scream and suddenly, the car no longer had a driver because Lavon was busy trying to crawl across the top of Larry to get out through the passenger's door. I guess Larry figured Lavon had done gone berserk and run amok.

I don't remember how many times the car straddled the ditch as we went around a curve and headed up Wilson Hill because I was sort of busy hanging on for dear life. The combined efforts of Larry and Junior finally got the car under control and brought us to a shuddering stop.

Of course, we all literally fell over with laughter while we re-lived this little episode. It was a good half hour before we could continue on home. They made me drive. For some reason, they wanted me to be securely in one spot with something to do. Those guys wanted to know exactly where I was and what I was doing at all times.

Well, we were a bunch of pretty lucky kids. We got into a lot of wild and crazy situations while we were growing up. Amazingly enough, none of us used alcohol or drugs. We didn't even smoke. Which is probably a good thing. We already got into so much foolishness, anyway, while we were straight and sober, can you imagine what might have happened if any of us had ever been drunk or stoned?

Anyway, we all survived that particular event and went on to have many other exciting escapades, most of which were just as dumb as this one and, except for a little dirt on the undercarriage, the car had come through basically undamaged. Except for those claw marks across the roof.

Chapter 14

Biker Dude

Let me tell you about my adventure as a biker dude. No, you didn't read incorrectly. That word, adventure, is in the singular sense. It only took ONE to convince me that I would never be the Marlon Brando type, leading a gang of leather-jacketed tough guys and biker-chicks across the countryside.

Now, my adventure didn't involve one of those Harley Davidson "hogs" or any of those other macho-type motorcycles. It was a Honda. Not a big one, either. A Honda 50. My sister's Honda 50. Shirley's toy.

Okay, see, back in the days when she was a newspaper reporter, she used it to get around to accident scenes and other events where a big old car was too much trouble. She even got to using it for chores and errands, like doing shopping and taking the kids around.

Well, it was the summer of 1973. My wife, Juanita, and I were visiting with Shirley's family one weekend and I asked her if I could try out her little toy. She said yes because she figured what could possibly go wrong. After all, I was a big bad Marine Corps Sergeant, already famous for my daring deeds and exploits. This would be the very least of my challenges.

Well, she found out. So did I. I had ridden off, smiling happily, the wind blowing in my face, enjoying the little toy. Some two hours later, I returned, no longer smiling, clothing torn and ragged, dirty, cut, bruised, limping…pushing the demon bike.

Shirley was horrified. I didn't want to tell her what had happened but she forced it out of me by threatening to take me for another ride on that evil, bewitched, possessed two-wheeled monster if I didn't tell her the story.

Things had started out just fine. I went through all the gears, made a few nice curves, even managed to take one hand off the handlebars a couple of times to wave at folks along the way. Then, IT happened.

Shirley lived in Adona, at that time, and I hadn't gone too far out of town on Hwy 10 when I decided to turn around. I pulled off into a cemetery parking lot. Lo and behold, it was a GRAVELLED parking lot. Except for a couple of homemade bicycles I had when I was a kid, I was relatively inexperienced at handling two-wheeled critters on gravel so it came as a considerable surprise when the motorcycle slid out from under me.

I was sort of half off and half on that beast, I had lost my grip with one hand, it was still in gear and the only thing I had a hold on was the THROTTLE. I don't understand why I was determined to stay with that bike but I didn't let go and it started turning circles in that gravel. Dragging me with it.

I don't know how many circles we made in that gravel. Cut out a pretty good groove, though. After losing a considerable amount of skin and after I had tiny bits of gravel permanently embedded in several major portions of my anatomy, it did finally occur to me that this particular form of insanity and self-abuse could cease if I would just LET GO of the bike. So I did. Thus ended my one and only adventure as a biker-dude.

Chapter 15

Snake Dancer

Yes, I was once a snake dancer. Sort of. But it ain't what you're probably thinking.

It was along about August of 1976. Juanita and I were living on the Marine base in Albany, Georgia. Right across the fence from our back yard was a swamp (No, not the famous Okeefenokee) and one day around noontime, I found a big old copperhead snake on the back porch. Not that I was looking for one. The discovery was quite a surprise for both of us. I promptly fell backward over a chair, which excited the snake, so he decided to head for parts unknown.

I was determined to avoid the prospect of any future visitations by this particular uninvited guest, so I quickly held court, found him guilty of trespassing and sentenced him to termination with extreme prejudice (that's military talk for I was gonna kill him). I came off the floor with the first object I could grab, which was a hoe. We do-si-do'ed across the porch a couple of times, sashayed down the steps, waltzed around the end of the house once or twice and jitterbugged all over most of the backyard.

Sometimes he would lead and sometimes I would lead. The neighbors were watching this spectacle and were really enjoying the show. I may not be another Gene Kelly or John Travolta but I must say, I displayed quite a few pretty good moves. Considering the garden implement I had chanced upon with which I intended to effect my dance partner's untimely demise, you could say it was a regular HOE-down.

Luckily, the dance finally came to an end and I was able to swing my partner limply back across the fence into the flora from which he had come. As I walked slowly and wearily back across the yard, dragging my hoe (and various body parts) behind me, one of my neighbors called over to me with a startling observation, "You know, they usually travel in pairs". As I looked apprehensively around for the critter that might be waiting to pick up where the other one had left off, I realized….the dance had only just begun.

Chapter 16

Close Encounter

On 29 June 1994, my brother-in-law, Dennis, and I had a "Close Encounter of the Third Kind". No, we didn't meet any wildlife, aliens, creatures of the night or see Elvis. We had a run-in with a soft drink vending machine that did not want to surrender its contents.

We wrestled around with it for a couple of minutes before we succeeded in obtaining even one soda pop. I, being the older human, decided to claim that one. However, I very graciously offered to assist him in his efforts to obtain a drink of his own. Partially out of the goodness of my heart, of course. And partially out of concern for the way he kept looking at my soda.

The lights of the machine went out so we decided that the electrical receptacle had come unplugged. While Dennis walked the machine out of the corner, I sandwiched my-self between the machine and the wall, trying to get my hand on the cord. I got it. It was plugged in. Then I really got it. An electric jolt went into my hand, through my body and out to my other hand, which was still holding the first soda.

I invented a new dance, on the spot. Choreographed it, too, right then and there. Called it the Static Stomp. It consisted of uttering a vocal imitation of my favorite Disney cartoon character (which means I did a Goofy yell), dancing wildly in place while jiggling an open soda pop in one hand.

When the dance was over, there was a lot of fluid on the floor at my feet. I hereby wish to establish and maintain one fact: That liquid came from that opened soda pop can and from nowhere else.

Dennis decided to skip the soda machine and had some coffee, instead.

Chapter 17

Order to go

During June 1994, I was spending some time at my sister's place (Luvbilt Crafts) north of Dover. On a lazy Friday evening, Shirley and Dennis were gone to a pickin' and grinnin' and I was there by myself. I'm not allowed to be alone in a kitchen without adult supervision. I think that's by federal law. If you have ever seen the results when I have tried to cook, you will understand why that law was passed. Even without meaning to, I become Public Enemy # 1 and a threat to life on this planet whenever I'm in a kitchen.

But I was hungry so I decided to drive down to Dover for some food. I went to the walk-up window at the Pirates' Cove diner and ordered a hamburger and fries to go. I told the girl I was going to pick up a few things at a store while waiting for my order and would return shortly.

I finished my shopping and drove leisurely back to the house. I planned to watch a movie while I ate. I got the vcr loaded with a Laurel and Hardy movie titled *Way Out West* and settled in for the evening. That was when I realized I didn't have my food. My order-to-go didn't get to go when I went because I drove right by the Cove without even thinking about it.

I drove the eight miles back to Dover, whipped into the parking lot and sauntered over to the window where I asked, just as nonchalantly as you please, "Say, Ma'am, do you reckon my order to go is ready to go, yet?". Uh, yes, it was.

I hate old age. I've lost my hair, my hearing, my eyesight, my boyish charm, my manly figure, my memory and my wits.

Chapter 18

Slow Sand

In August 1994, we had just moved into a trailer on the south side of Atkins. Since I am a stickler for details, I had bought some stick-on letters for the mailbox to assert the identity of the new tenants.

I was standing in the ditch, sticking on the letters and humming a little tune to myself. (I always have my music with me, except when something happens to make me lose my music). As I worked, I noticed something peculiar. Was it my imagination or was the mailbox and post growing taller and taller? Yes, by the time I had finished the job, that mailbox had pert' near grown half a foot taller. But when I tried to move, I discovered that it wasn't the mailbox that was growing but myself that was shrinking. Well, okay, actually sinking, not shrinking. I couldn't move my feet. I had sunk down into a mire that was reluctant to let me go.

After I finally got out of the bog, I reasoned that if it had been some QUICK sand instead of SLOW sand, I might have realized sooner that I was being taken in. Then, I wouldn't have ruined my shoes and made a mess of my pants. With the mud, I mean.

Chapter 19

Show-Off Button

During November 1994, I was clearing a fence line along Hwy 247 in Economy early one morning. It was misty and everything was pretty wet. I didn't have my favorite gloves with me and was having to use a pair that was a little too big.

I had a pretty good pile of brush built up and I was working close enough to the road so that I could see the occupants of the vehicles that went by. I saw a car approaching that had two pretty girls in it and my macho, show-off button clicked on.

I picked up a log that LOOKED very heavy (but actually wasn't), heaved it into the air and tossed it toward the brush pile. Well, one of my oversized gloves, which had become quite wet, slipped off my hand and went sailing clean over the brush pile.

While hoping to cover up that little blunder, I quickly picked up a batch of briars and brambles with the other hand and flung it toward the brush pile. Well, one of the briars caught hold of my cap as it whipped overhead and took my cap right along with it into the brush pile.

I stood there dumbfounded for a moment while my audience drove away, giggling. Then, I realized that it was probably a lucky thing for me that I didn't happen to have anything else handy to throw. The way things were going, I was losing an article of clothing with every swing and before too long, I could have wound up buck naked. So I promptly turned off my show-off button and started CARRYING things to the brush pile.

Chapter 20

Liquid or Solid

By January 1995, I had evolved through life into the type of person who caught a cold in October and kept it until April. I hadn't been that way at all until 1983, when I had taken off my Marine Corps officer's uniform and put on civilian clothing. It was like changing from Superman into Clark Kent. I became an instant wimp. The ravages of rapidly advancing old age may also have had something to do with it.

At the time of this incident, I was living in Atkins and working in Clarksville. The commute wasn't too bad, what with the interstate and all, and I was carpooling with a coworker named Danny. He and his wife are the kindly, caring type of folks and they had taken pity on me because I had a really bad cough.

I had been taking some of those 12-hour tablets but I had run out of them, having taken the last one on the way home one evening after work. The next morning, when Danny picked my up, he told me his wife had sent me something for my cold.

He handed me one of those little dark-colored pill bottles. I expected it to be a couple of cold capsules or pills like I had been taking, so I popped the lid off and tilted the bottle to pour one of them into my palm. But she had put some of their LIQUID cough syrup in there, instead.

We had just pulled onto the interstate with a half-hour trip ahead of us so I had no choice but to lick that stuff off of my hand while trying not to gag. See, I have an awful hard time trying to take liquid cough syrup because most of it has a little alcohol in it--and I never drank in my life. Usually, I have to take several deep breaths before I down a spoonful of cough syrup because after I suck up some of that stuff, it takes me a minute or so to get my breath back.

So there I was, having to lick up that stuff off of my hand a little at a time. Boy howdy, it just about killed me. I would have preferred to have the cough rather than the cure, but I didn't want to seem like an ingrate. I learned my lesson. Ever since then, I check everything to see if it is in liquid or solid form.

Chapter 21

Demon Sweat Bee

During April 1995, there I was, clearing another fence line. It was hot so I was working with my shirt off. Things went pretty well, for a while. Then, I heard the steady drone of little wings. Now, most of y'all can probably relate to being bothered by sweat bees. I've had plenty of them to get after me before, but this was the DEMON SWEAT BEE FROM HADES.

It wasn't bad enough that he was dive-bombing me but he would wait until I had an armload of brush and limbs before he would come after me. It went on, all morning long. Whenever I figured that he had headed for parts unknown, he would show up and take a bite. Always when I least expected it. Always when my arms were full. Always from the back.

I took a full hour for my lunch break, hoping that the DEMON SWEAT BEE would move on or find some other victim in my absence. Wrong. He apparently clocked out for lunch the same time I did and was back on the job the same time I was.

The rest of the day was miserable. We were practically inseparable. By the end of the day, I was pert' near exhausted--not from the work but from my encounters with the DEMON SWEAT BEE.

Well, I finally got into my truck for the ride home, still with my shirt off. Lo and behold, the DEMON SWEAT BEE came in through the open window for just one more attack. But this time, he made the mistake of landing on my chest where I could see him. With a quick swat, I put an end to my arch-enemy. With no remorse, whatsoever. As I crossed Gum Log Creek on the way home, I flipped him out the window off the bridge toward the water with this thought:

I no longer have to flee
He'll never again get me
It's burial at sea
For the DEMON SWEAT BEE

Chapter 22

Don't Look, Ethel

During June 1995, I was doing a little cleanup around a house on Hwy 247 in the Economy community. I was working in a particularly brushy area, pulling out scraps of metal and other junk when I came across the discarded hood of a truck.

Being the outdoorsy type of guy that I am, I just knew instinctively that it would be the perfect place for a critter to have a den or for a wasp nest. So I carefully kicked the hood. Nothing happened. I kicked harder. Still nothing. Just to be on the safe side, I jumped up on the hood and danced around a little while humming a tune. Nothing. Thoroughly convinced that I would have scared off anything that might have been under there, I picked up the hood. There, standing on his hind legs, ready for battle, was a big old badger. I hadn't scared him off--I had just made him mad.

I was no longer humming my tune. I hate it when I lose my music. It doesn't happen very often but when it does happen, it's usually in situations quite similar to this one. So I dropped the hood and headed for parts unknown. It was an official one-Roy stampede. I have no idea where the badger went.

Later on that day, I was mowing the grass on the other side of the house. At one point, I had seen a snake wandering off through the grass so I was on my guard. In fact, I had even regained my music.

Suddenly, I felt something crawling up the inside of my britches leg. I didn't take time to run around behind the house. I didn't check to see if any cars were going by. I simply did my own version of the Ray Stevens Streak without even taking time to holler, "Don't look, Ethel".

With my britches around my ankle, I discovered that it was only a lizard, who was probably just as scared as I was. Pert' near had another one-Roy stampede. And I had once again lost my music.

Chapter 23

Friendly Fellers

During July 1995, Robert and I were cutting some limbs off an old dead tree out behind my apartment. The limbs were over a power line and we knew that if we didn't take them out, the next storm would blow them down, taking the power line with them and deprive my family of electricity. They were leaning pretty far in the wrong direction so I had to climb up and tie a rope to them so Robert could pull them in the preferred direction while I sawed on them. We got a couple of limbs down in this manner but one limb was a lot heavier than Robert, or maybe it was just tougher.

So, we backed my old truck around there and tied the limb to the back bumper. That worked better. As I cut, Robert kept tension on the limb by pulling with the truck. It fell about where I wanted it to. Afterward, we loaded the brush and limbs onto the truck. Then, we threw the ladder on top of the load, intending to return it to where we had borrowed it before we took the load to the pasture.

We hopped into the truck and took off. A lot of people waved at us and a few who were in cars honked at us. We smiled and waved back at everybody. We're friendly fellers. When we unloaded the ladder, we noticed that we had forgotten to untie the rope from the bumper. We had driven through Atkins dragging a 20-foot rope with a hook on the end of it. No wonder people were waving and honking at us. It's a good thing we didn't hook a sign or a fence or a culvert....or a pedestrian.

By the way, Atkins had a severe storm the very next day. A completely different tree had fallen across the power line so we were without electricity, anyway. I went to borrow a chain saw and a ladder. No ropes or hooks, this time.

Before we had the electricity hooked back up, I did my Paul Bunyan imitation and cut down everything that might have any chance at all of hitting the power line in the future. By the time I was finished, there wasn't anything dead left in the backyard. Except me.

Chapter 24

Rough Day at Work

During July 1995, I had a rough day at work. At the warehouse where I was employed, the trucker's lounge was separated from the receiving section by that type of door that is divided in the middle so you could open either the top half or the bottom half by itself. Usually, these halves were bolted together. That day, they weren't. Well, I went dashing into the lounge. At least, I started to dash. Moving at a high rate of speed,

I grabbed the door handle, pushed on the door and kept going. The top half opened but the bottom half remained firmly closed. Now, I'm not tall enough to do a complete flip over that half-door but I was exactly tall enough to become intimately familiar with the door knob of that bottom half. There I was, suspended across that barrier with both ends swinging free like yesterday's laundry on the line, flapping in the breeze. A couple of the drivers asked me if I was alright and I told them I was just fine but I don't really think they believed me. Maybe it was that high squeaky falsetto voice that came out of me that damaged my credibility.

Later that day, I went through that door again, grabbed the OTHER door knob and started through. I came within an inch of slamming my face into the top half of the door, which had stayed shut. Luckily, I'm old enough to remember Chubby Checker and his hit song, *Limbo Rock*. No, I did not attempt to limbo completely under that half-door but I was once quite a gymnast and I was a limbo quasi-champion, so I was able to "assume the position" quickly enough and for long enough to avoid kissing the door.

Chapter 25

Roger Miller Bug

I've always had a soft spot in my heart for small animals. I can poison roaches and rats or swat mosquitoes and sweat bees with no qualms but I almost cry if I should accidentally run over some little critter on the road.

Well, one day, I was getting ready to shave. I had just filled my palm with shaving cream and just as I dabbed the shaving cream on my face, a miller bug (later dubbed the Roger Miller Bug) landed on my palm and got dabbed on my face.

I was determined to save the little critter, so I peeled him off my face and laid him on a paper towel. I had to use a washrag to pat off the shaving cream but when I finally got it all off of him, his wings were still wet so he couldn't fly away.

I wanted to dry him off but I didn't have anything like a blow dryer. However, there was an old curling iron in the cabinet so I turned it on and laid it next to him. All was going well until I discovered I had Roger Miller Bug lying too close to the curling iron and his little wings were…well…curling. I made an adjustment and he was soon able to fly. Which he did.

Chapter 26

High Stuff

Shirley's husband, Dennis, doesn't like getting high. No, no, not that kind of high. He doesn't drink or use drugs at all. I mean, he doesn't like getting into or onto high places. So imagine my surprise when I went up there to visit along about September 1995 and found him on top of the Playroom. Actually, it's a lot more than just a room. It's a rather large structure where they hold their Bluegrass festivals during inclement weather.

He was on top of it, cutting a hole for a stove pipe for a heater he was setting up in the playroom. I don't know what kind of power tool he was using but he kept asking for more blades. When his partner, Louie, told him he had only two new blades left, Dennis said, "Well, give me some of the old blades. I'll re-use them". I never did get an exact count of the blades he had gone through but it must have been in the double digits.

He only had to cut about an 8-inch hole. Maybe he should have just gotten rid of the power tool he was using and tried a hand powered hacksaw because every time he would fire up that power tool and start cutting, it would vibrate him and he would get the impression he was falling and would try to find something to grab hold of and that would mess up his aim and break the blade. Dennis was still up there when I left. Of course, I was only there for a few hours.

However, I shouldn't be too hard on Dennis. I'm not exactly fond of high places, myself. When I lived in North Carolina, I tried hang gliding. Once. Had plenty of pre-flight training. But you don't really need training. All you need is to be crazy.

There I was, strapped to a mechanical device. It wasn't enough that I was on top of a very high hill. As if the hill wasn't already high enough, they had built a ramp on top of the hill to make it even higher. And it wasn't bad enough that I had to jump off the end of the ramp on top of that hill, no, I had to RUN down the ramp as if I really WANTED to go. And to think I actually paid good money for the experience.

An instructor went up the hill with me. I told him to take a gun with him. He assured me that there were no wild animals in the area and that he wouldn't need a gun. I said, "Oh, yes, you will definitely need a gun to make me run down and jump off the end of that ramp".

When we got up there, I was concerned because there were some big old rocks on the side of the hill just below the end of the ramp. The instructor said not to worry--those rocks would be the least of my worries. That did not exactly reassure me. If those rocks were the least of my worries, what would be the most of my worries? However, every-thing worked the way it was supposed to. I was airborne before I got halfway down the ramp.

I must point out that I wasn't allowed to fly free wherever I wanted because there was a small anchor rope (kind of like a kite string) that wouldn't let me do that. I had to fly straight forward and land in a field about half a mile away. There was an interstate high-way on the other side of the field and they didn't want any amateurs landing in front of a semi-truck. Well, I wouldn't have wanted to land in front of a semi-truck even if I was a professional so I didn't mind that particular restriction.

The instructor's partner was waiting in the field to assist with my landing. I wondered how he was going to do that. I was pretty sure he wasn't going to try to catch me. But the landing went well. I floated in and started running, as instructed, as soon as my feet hit the ground, intending to slow down gradually so I wouldn't take a nosedive. Not to worry. I'm probably the only student who came in for a landing and actually picked up speed when I touched down. I always was a good jogger.

I had done some rappelling, too, during a different time when I was living in North Carolina, but that was while I was stationed at Camp Lejeune as a Marine Corps Platoon Commander and it was in the course of regular training with my platoon, so there was nothing remarkable about that.

However, I also tried bungee jumping during that period of time, which was not part of platoon training. It was at sort of a carnival thing, which was a local annual event. It was off the end of about a 40-foot crane, which wasn't any higher than the tower that we had rappelled from. After I got in line for the bungee jump, there was no way I was going to step OUT of line because some of my platoon members were there. And after I had climbed up to the top of that crane, there was no way I was going to climb back down. I got hooked up and jumped off. It was sort of a compulsory macho insanity situation. I didn't mind having my platoon members think I was crazy but I didn't want them to know I was afraid.

I've topped a few trees with a chain saw and I've enjoyed a bit of tame rock climbing on some of the local bluffs here in Pope County but the last time I got high (I mean, in a high place) was when I was helping E. Ray tear down an old house on his property in Russellville.

On a rainy Monday morning, we were removing the roofing material. As we tore up the roofing material and tarpaper, those little grainy, pebbly, sandy-type thingies were coming off the tarpaper. They were everywhere up there. What with the misty rain and those little grainy thingies, the roof was pretty slick.

Quite often, one of us would stand up a little too straight or put our weight a little too far back on our heels, which would cause us to go surfing down across the roof, Neither one of us went so far as to take a nosedive over the edge but we had some scary moments. Obviously, we were not professional roofers. Or should I say, de-roofers.

Chapter 27

WD-40

It was sometime in October 1995 that I decided that Dennis was in a lot better shape than I was. I knew he was pretty strong but I didn't know how strong until I bought an old truck from him. The first time I tried to check the oil, I thought I was going to have to crawl underneath to get to the dipstick. I could NOT raise the hood. Oh, I could get the catch to release but getting the hood up was a different matter. Those springs and hinges were TIGHT. I though I was going to have to get a crowbar, a 2 x 4 and an axle jack to raise that hood. I figured that, after a few months of opening and closing that hood, I could compete for the Mr. Universe title.

I've never been accused of being the most brilliant thing in the world but I figured this was a problem I could solve. I could make those springs and hinges looser. With WD-40 About a gallon of WD-40. And it worked, by golly. For someone of my advanced years and deteriorated physical condition, opening and closing that hood was finally within the realm of possibilities.

However, I did make one small oversight when I fixed the hood--I forgot to tell good old Dennis. There came a time when I needed to replace the points and set the timing on the truck. Okay, the truth is, I needed for Dennis to do that stuff. I'm not mechanical, at all. I can put gas and oil in but that's about the extent of my automotive abilities. And water-I know where to put the water.

So, imagine Dennis's surprise when he jerked the hood open with all his strength, as he had been accustomed to doing, in the past. It flew all the way open, then slammed back down. The look on his face! He opened it again, very slowly and carefully, and pushed it all the way up. He looked at the hood, warily. Then he looked at me, just as warily, and said, "This USED to be a good truck. What have you DONE to it?". After I told him, he went back to work on the distributor, muttering something under his breath about amateurs and weaklings.

Chapter 28

Wood Splitting and Hay Hauling

During the spring of 1996, I made a depressing discovery. I found out that I had pert' near forgot how to split wood. I always figured it was like riding a bicycle. Boy, did I get a rude awakening. A neighbor in Economy named Kenneth Ennis asked me to split some wood for him. He and his beautiful wife, Wanda Jean, had helped raise me so I didn't hesitate for a second.

He loaned me his splitting mawl and I headed for the woods. Now, I'm not going to say that these pieces of wood were as big around as a kitchen table but if you put one of them on MY table, there wouldn't be enough room for a plate. The mawl was about a 12-pounder but it also had a large metal handle so I was at least smart enough to realize that I should make every swing count.

When I took my first swing, I expected to hear a dull thunk as the mawl bit into the wood but what I heard was a sharp clear ping, like metal on metal. I checked the block of wood. It was only wood. Not metal. But I could barely tell where I had hit the block.

Back in the early 1960's, my famous swing would have bit deeply into that block, causing a large split to run completely across the top of the block. There was barely an indentation where the mawl had hit. I took another swing. Ping, again. And, much to my surprise, I had not hit anywhere near the first mark. My aim was way off. What was the deal here? Did this block of wood actually have no idea of WHO I was? Roy, the Master Wood Splitter. Why, the very mention of my name should have caused cracks to appear across the tops of most of those blocks. For some reason, that was not happening.

After 20 more swings, I had 20 more tiny indentations all over the top of that block. No split had appeared. I hadn't hit the same place, twice. Had I lost my aim? Had I lost my magic touch? Was I truly no longer the "swinger" of yesteryear? Folks, it's a good thing I was alone in the woods. It isn't a pretty sight when a legend dies. I got that wood split but it took a tiny bit longer than I thought it would. I even remember the thrill of excitement that ran through me when I finally hit the same place, twice in a row. It was 10:27 on a Sunday morning. I toasted that first block of wood with a couple of sips from my soda pop.

Unfortunately, that wasn't the only depressing discovery I had made around that time. I had been waiting patiently for my first chance in many years to get back into some hay hauling. Most everybody had started baling those big round bales that have to be handled by a tractor with a hydraulic fork on the front. However, Ezell Johnston (of Economy) baled 1,000 square bales and got me to haul them.

When I was a kid, I usually hauled hay by myself, 53 bales to a load on my old pickup truck. Now, some of y'all may not believe this but, when I was a teenager, I could throw a bale of hay over the top of my loaded truck, from the ground. Those of you who knew me back in the good old days will remember that I did that very thing many times. What happened? It took me by surprise to realize that hauling that 1,000 bales of hay was actually going to require some serious effort, on my part, when it should have been just about like a walk in the park. I have hauled some more square bales, since then, but that first 1,000 bales just about broke my heart. Not to mention my back.

Chapter 29

A Giant of a Man

Ezell Johnston was a man that I had known since I was just a little kid. Two of his sons are my lifelong best friends. He was a giant of a man. During his younger years, they could have used him in some of those muscleman movies they made in the 1960's with Steve Reeves or Gordon Scott playing the part of Hercules.

During April of 1996, I was helping him clear out an old fence from around the yard of his sister-in-law's place. It was a metal link fence with metal poles. All of the poles had concrete bases on them and had already been pulled out of the ground with the use of a tractor. I was picking up the poles and loading them onto a trailer while Ezell drove.

Those poles were heavy! I was grunting and straining and broke a pretty good sweat after only 6 or 7 poles. I was getting behind, so he hopped off the tractor to help. I said, "Now, watch out, they're pretty heavy". He reached down with one hand, picked up a pole with a big concrete base on it, lifted it over the sideboard of the trailer and set it down. Then he said, "Yeah, they do have a little weight to them".

Folks, if you had seen the height and size of Ezell, you might not think it was quite so remarkable that he would be able to handle those poles like that. But at that time, he was in his 70's. He had also had heart surgery. And about a year before this, he had been accidentally shot in the back with a shotgun from a distance of just a few feet. Y'all, that is what I call old-timey tough. I'd sure hate to get a feller like that mad at me. And I would not want to ever go after him with anything less than a machine gun or a bazooka.

Luckily, he was one of the good guys. I've been fortunate to have known a lot of folks like that while I was growing up. There seemed to be a lot of that type around in our neck of the woods back in the good old days. Seems like they have just about quit making them like that, anymore.

Chapter 30

Come Along

During May 1996, Atkins had recently had an extended period of heavy rain, so I had to drive my truck through my back yard where, true to form, I got it thoroughly stuck. Up to the axle. It wasn't stuck up to the axle, from the start. I had to work at it for awhile before I got it that deep. Initially, I just couldn't get quite enough traction to pull out of a low spot in the back corner and things just escalated from there.

First, I tried to put some small boards under the back wheels to use as tiny ramps to get a running start. The tires spun up onto the boards. One of the boards got pushed into the ground so deep, I decided to let future archeologists worry about it. The other board, which apparently had a rough spot on it, shot out behind the truck several feet. I promptly abandoned that idea.

Next, I tried digging out from under the tires so I could make sort of a ramp to get a run up. The holes filled up with water so fast, pretty soon all I was shoveling was water. And the truck was sinking steadily deeper.

Then I decided to jack up the truck so I could fill in under the tires with small rocks. The truck didn't rise any but the jack settled pretty deep in the ground. I tried putting a block of wood under the jack. The jack and the block of wood both settled down into the ground together.

I had only two choices left. I discarded one of the choices immediately because I did not want to turn my truck into a permanent backyard flower planter. The other choice was to borrow a vehicle and then go borrow a come-along from Ezell Johnston, out in Economy. That was two "borrows" at one time and it was sort of embarrassing, but I did it. I also got a 20-foot logging chain from Kenneth Ennis. I sure was racking up a lot of "borrows".

In case you don't know what a come-along is, I will just have to describe it because I have never heard it called anything else. It's sort of a block-and-tackle device that has a cable that gets wound up onto a rotating spool as you crank a handle which turns the spool. The cable has a hook on it. The come-along also has a short chain with a hook on its other end. Some of them have just a hook on the other end with no chain. Anyway, when you anchor that hook to a big rock or a tree and start cranking that handle, whatever you have that hook on the cable end hooked to is going to come-along. Hence, the name.

Well, I anchored that come-along to a big old tree and hooked the cable end to the truck and started cranking that handle. That cable got so tight, you could practically pluck a tune on it, the anchor chain was biting deep into that tree and the handle was so rigid, I couldn't crank it another notch…but the truck had never moved. I was certain that I had everything hooked up correctly. I checked the tires. They weren't up against any obstructions. That old truck should have come-along-ed several feet, by that time.

Then a thought struck me. With a brain like mine, thoughts don't strike me very often but I do have my little moments. This thought made me go over to the truck and take it out of gear. After that, the truck moved along fairly well. I took up the slack twice while anchored to that tree but the truck was still too far back in the yard to get traction.

I moved the come-along and anchored it to another tree closer to the corner of the house. I thought after two or three more times of taking up the slack in the cable, I would have the truck far enough out of the marshy area to get some traction.

I started cranking. After taking up nearly all of the slack in the cable, I realized that the truck was not moving…again. I didn't have to check it this time. I KNEW that truck was out of gear. But it should have moved six or seven feet by this time and the handle had never got tight. I had been cranking right along. Where had all that slack gone? I walked around the truck and pondered for awhile. Then I just happened to look at the tree. It was leaning at least a 45-degree angle toward the truck.

I froze. That thing looked ominous. I very carefully unhooked from the tree. Then I got a friend to back his car up to the corner of the house where he would still have some traction. Then I used that long logging chain to reach between the two vehicles. He couldn't pull me out but with his car as an anchor, I come-along-ed the truck out of the backyard. That old tree had been hollow and was pert' near dead so we eventually cut it up into firewood. From the time I pulled into the backyard until I finally got out was from 6:00 pm until 10:30 pm.

Folks, I have used tractors with hoists to pull trees down. I have used chain saws, crosscut saws, handsaws, axes, hatchets and machetes to cut trees down. I have pushed trees down with trucks and tractors and even with my bare hands. But that was the first time I had ever come-along-ed a tree down.

Chapter 31

Fence Work

By June 1996, I had been doing a lot of fence work since spring. I cleared them, tore them down, built them and painted them. Now, to tear down a fence, I usually use a hammer, a fencing tool and a pair of leather gloves. Except for this one time.

Okay, it was like this. I got off work at Russellville long after midnight and headed home with my co-worker/co-rider, John. My old truck was broken down at the time and we were in a borrowed car. Alright, east of Atkins, there are two dirt roads that turn to the left from Hwy 64 and cross over the interstate. The first road crosses the interstate and immediately comes to a T, where you have to turn either left or right. The second road crosses the interstate and runs straight for a long, long way. To get John home, I was supposed to take the second dirt road.

Well, it was the middle of the night, I was very tired, it was foggy as pea soup and I thought I knew where I was. I turned off on the wrong road, went charging up over the interstate, dashed down the other side and gunned the motor, expecting a long, straight run. Suddenly, I was at a T and had no more road--not straight in front of me, anyway.

I slammed on the brakes but that had little effect. The car jumped the ditch, ran up a bank and went through a fence. It was barbed wire and it broke clean. I hooked a circle in the pasture and drove back over to the fence. We couldn't get back out the way we had come in because the ditch had a bank on the wrong side.

I drove down to the corner of the pasture, where John opened a gate for me and we got back on the road. John knew the folks who owned the place and told me it would be okay until morning.

Next day, bright and early, I took my tools and some new wire that I had left over from one of my recent fence-building projects and went over there to fix that fence. I got it done and nobody came out of the house to shoot me. That was a good thing.

So, if any of y'all have a fence you want torn down, just let me know because I am very experienced. However, if you don't mind, I'll work off of the back end of my truck instead of off the front end of a borrowed car because the person who had loaned me the car told me not to use this particular method of tearing out fences, any more. She told me some other stuff, too. But I can't print it.

A few days later, I was tearing out a fence on the Johnston Farm in Economy. Yes, I had my truck and I was using my regular fencing tools that day. But this particular fence ran through a fish pond, made a corner in the middle of the pond near an old stump and a beaver dam and went out the other side. I wasn't surprised. I wasn't dismayed. I wasn't perturbed. What I was, was wet.

Yes, friends and neighbors, I was not to be denied. My fence tearer-downer reputation was at stake. Where that fence went, I would follow. The pond wasn't there when the fence was built years ago but that didn't make any difference to me. I would have made a good postman, huh? Neither rain, nor snow, nor sleet, nor fish ponds would keep me from my appointed rounds. That fence had met its match. Roy, the Master Fence Dude.

Removing the wire was the hard part. The fence was a combination of iron poles and old cedar posts. From the front side, I didn't get out more than neck-deep. I removed the wire a section at a time and carried it to shore. Then, I floated the poles to shore one at a time. At least, I floated the ones that were made out of cedar to shore. I carried the metal poles because they wouldn't float, for some reason. Finally, there were only four poles left from the front side and they were in an area that would be over my head, so I decided to work from the other side for a while.

I waded out and made it to the old stump by climbing across the beaver dam, taking the top strand loose from the poles as I waded out.

Then I used the same procedure of removal that I had used on the front side.

I then took a rowboat, (which I had not seen until that very moment) out to the deep part to get those last four poles. The wire was loose at both ends, so it wasn't so bad. I worked the poles loose and pulled them into the boat, one at a time. Pert' near turned the boat over, twice. Wound up with a jumble of poles and wire in the boat but that pond was clear. It was a good job. Different. Didn't have to pull any briars or brambles out of the fence before tearing it out. Didn't have to worry much about poison ivy, either.

But you know, the whole time I was wading around out there in the middle of that pond with the stump and the beaver dam and the waterweeds and a few old dead trees hanging over me, I was kind of scared. No, no, I wasn't scared of angry beavers, water moccasins, snapping turtles or six-foot, two hundred pound, man-eating catfish. Nope.

I was worried about the Swamp Creature, the Boggy Creek Monster and the Creature from the Black Lagoon. Might as well throw in the Wolfman, too, because late in the evening, the shadows got pretty long and the cattle were restless.

Anyway, if you have a fence you want torn down, whether I have to use the front end of a borrowed car, a boat, or just simply work off the back of my old truck, I am the man for the job. Just don't expect me to stay out there on the job too long after dark. That's when the vampires come out.

Chapter 32

Modern Technology

During September 1996, I was almost a victim of modern technology. A nice new fence was put up around part of the Johnston property. After I had pulled out the briars and brambles, cut the brush and weeds, removed all of the old fence and helped paint the new fence, I wrote an article about the new fence in which I claimed that it was so clean we could keep it cleared with a lawn mower, if the boss wanted us to. Well, Gerald just about took me at my word.

He found a machine that made me and my weed cutter (a swing blade) obsolete. That thing looked like a hay mowing sickle mounted on the front of a self-propelled chassis with handlebars sticking out the back. Those handlebars are the only thing that kept me from being phased out of my fence-clearing job. The machine needed a human being (or in my case, a reasonable facsimile) to hold those handlebars. That thing cut a 42-inch wide swath and would take down just about anything except telephone poles and the metal poles that held up the fence. I cleared every bit of that new fence, front and back, in 13 hours. That included hooking a trailer onto my old truck, loading and unloading, and transport time.

What with overlapping and inexperience, I cut at least a six-foot area on both sides of the fence and, by the time I finished, I had only one request. I wanted somebody to get modern technology to help me train those cows so they wouldn't deposit any more cow patties within six feet of the fence.

Chapter 33

Common Sense

During September 1996, I took a friend to the emergency room at a hospital in Morrilton late one evening after he stepped on a nail. I figured that was a good time to take him there because I would have been hard-pressed to explain what we were doing there if I took him before he stepped on a nail.

So I was sitting in the hallway outside one of their treatment rooms while his foot was soaking and I was totally bored. Didn't have anything to read--I can't sit still for five minutes without something to read. So I read the eye chart. It wasn't very entertaining, though. I couldn't make head or tails out of it. It didn't have a very good plot. So I looked around for something else to read.

I noticed a box of disposable face masks attached to the wall, presumably for the doctors and nurses to wear while they treated patients with infectious diseases. Y'all, that box had directions for use printed on the its side. Yeah, directions for putting the face mask on AND for taking it off. There might conceivably be someone out there dumb enough that he might not know how to put on a face mask but how could anybody in the world be dumb enough that he wouldn't be able to figure out how to take it back off?

I'm naïve enough to believe that doctors and nurses are supposedly relatively smart. In the first place, they have to finish high school. Then they go to college. Then they either go through nurse's training or medical school. Most of them also have to do a couple of years of internship. After all that education, training and experience, mightn't it be logical to assume that, by that time, they would have figured out how to put on and take off a face mask?

I would be willing to believe that the face mask manufacturer was required by the government to put those directions and instructive pictures on the box because I already know our beloved government thinks we're all a bunch of idiots and that we need these detailed instructions just to make it through the day. But wait a minute. It could also be that the people in the government are all idiots and they can't comprehend that other people might be smarter than they are.

Chapter 34

Ground Bees

During September 1996, I broke the speed record for land navigation. On foot. I was clearing a fence row on the back side of the Johnston farm. It was an old fence that had just recently come under Johnston responsibility. Portions of it had to be re-built, but that is another story.

Anyway, there I was, using my new chain saw to cut down saplings, vines and brush that had grown into and through the fence. At one point, I was working on one side of a tree that had grown on the fence line. Unknown to me, on the opposite side of the tree was an entrance hole of a nest where about a million ground bees lived.

The first hint I had of their presence was when the first one stung me, right on the little finger. That was very painful. It felt as if someone had stuck a match against my skin. It got my attention and served as a hint that I might be under attack by a group of ground bees. The fact that the air was instantly filled with ground bees was another subtle hint to that effect.

I immediately sold them the chain saw. Cheap. Then I headed for Parts Unknown. I figure I covered 120 yards in about 3 seconds. Yeah, I know that's impossible. Unless you are being attacked by ground bees. And I put on a pretty good show while covering that distance, too. Twisting around, flapping my arms, using my cap to try to slap those critters off of me. And of course, I had an audience for my performance. The bulldozer operators had arrived just in time.

Even after all the foot tapping, arm flapping and cap slapping, I had about 20 stings, which is actually a small number, considering the number of bees that were trying their best to get me. By the time I got home, I was feeling very sickly and had swelled up some. Turns out, I'm allergic to ground bees. A friend took me to the emergency room at the hospital in Morrilton. Yeah, wouldn't you know it, the same hospital where I had seen that box of disposable face masks that had directions (and pictures) on how to put on and take off face masks.

A physician examined me. I can only assume that he was a physician. He wasn't wearing a face mask but he did have a white lab coat and a stethoscope hanging from around his neck. After a careful examination, he decided that I had multiple stings. He had an uncanny ability to recognize the obvious, so I assumed that he had completed his internship. He advised me that I might feel sickly. That diagnosis and advice cost me $75.00. He told a nurse to give me a shot of diphenhydramine (50 mg). That amounted to an additional $46.20. And, of course, just walking into the emergency room cost me $45.00. The grand total was $166.20. Folks, that represents a lot of hours of fence clearing. And, dang, I had forgotten to charge admission to the dozer operators for the show. Furthermore, I still had to buy back my chain saw from those ground bees.

Chapter 35

Four Wheel Drive

During January 1997, I buried my truck in the mud, again. But this time, at least, it was not in the back yard. It was out in the woods. That seems more dignified, somehow. At least, it's the sort of place where one might actually even expect to get stuck, so it's not quite as embarrassing.

But I needed to haul some firewood. I had the tree down, trimmed and even split.

All I had to do was load it and haul it out. I got my old truck backed in there and loaded. When I tried to move the truck, it buried up to the frame. I had to unload the wood, jack the truck up a little at a time, stick wood under the wheels and then jack it up again. When I finally got the truck above ground, I still had to use a tractor to pull it out of the woods. But I still needed to get the wood out, so I parked the truck on a high spot in the pasture. I figured I could use the front end loader on the tractor to haul the firewood out and just dump it into the truck.

Well, it took about four tractor loads to get the firewood out that way. When I went back into the woods for that last little bit, doggone if I didn't get the tractor stuck. Folks, this was not a little tractor. This was a Rhino 5000. How could a guy stick a big old tractor like that? And that ain't the worst of it. It was a FOUR WHEEL DRIVE tractor. I buried it up to the frame. I just realized something--when I get something stuck, I really do a full job of it. No halfway efforts for me. When I stick something, it's always buried up to the frame, no matter what it is.

Anyway, I used the front bucket to shove against the ground to raise the front wheels out of the muck far enough so I could stick a few pieces of wood under them. Then I would get another bite with the bucket and raise the wheels again and shove more wood in there. I eventually worked my way out of the woods a little at a time, using that method.

Now, I know you're expecting me to tell you that I got the truck stuck again before I got out of the pasture but I didn't. Just pure dumb luck, I guess. You know, I'd bet that nobody else in the world could live my life for even one day without losing his mind. Who else but Roy could go into the woods with all that fancy equipment and wind up with about 40 pieces of good firewood irretrievably buried in the mud? That wood will never again see the light of day. A thousand years from now, archaeologists will wonder why there are pieces of wood buried in a crisscross pattern 5 or 6 feet deep underground. Maybe they will think it's some strange totem of an obscure indigenous local tribe. Yeah, a one-man tribe. A tribe called "Roy".

Chapter 36

Monday, Monday

The 29th of October in 2007 was the kind of Monday that gives Monday a bad name. First of all, it was cold and my fire had gone out overnight. I hate it when that happens. Sure, I could have got up sometime during the night to replenish the firewood in the stove but, hey, laziness happens every once in a while and, after all, I'm the one who had to pay the price. I could have built up a new fire but I would have been gone to work by the time the house got warm, anyway, so I didn't bother.

I had two choices for breakfast-I could choose to eat or not to eat. I chose to eat. Then, I had two choices regarding what to eat-eggs or corn flakes. If I chose eggs, I would have to actually USE the cook stove. I avoid that whenever possible, so I chose corn flakes.

Then, I discovered I was out of white milk but I had some chocolate milk, left over from the weekend when my nieces and nephew were visiting. I had never before had cereal with chocolate milk but I was not going to change my decision about what to eat. Besides, I had already poured the corn flakes and had sprinkled the imitation sugar all over them.

It wasn't long before I figured out why I had never before eaten cereal with chocolate milk. Folks, I don't recommend it. Actually, it might have been alright if I had been six years old--kids like weird stuff. But I was ten times six years old and, at that venerable age, chocolate milk just doesn't belong on corn flakes. Take my word for it.

So, I went to work. After I got my truck running, I turned on the windshield wipers to clear away the heavy dew but it wouldn't wipe off. It was frozen. I guess it had really got cold overnight. It took a few minutes of running the defroster before the wipers could get that stuff off.

At the farm, we discovered that the largest herd of cattle had got into a pasture where they didn't belong and were scattered over fifty acres. We all hopped on four wheelers to drive them back up.

It was still cold and the grass down there was very high so, as I went dashing about on the four wheeler my feet and legs got drenched by the frozen heavy dew. And as the front of the four wheeler ran against the tall grass, my face and upper body were showered by the ice crystals that got snapped off of the grass. I had a pair of insulated gloves but it was still an hour later before I could feel my fingers.

It eventually warmed up and turned into the first really bright, sunshiny day we'd had in a couple of weeks. I was going to be working outside all day so, naturally, the first thing I did was break my sunglasses. That was inevitable.

Later, I was running the tractor with a bush hog. I got stuck and had to get my boss to bring one of the other tractors to give me a pull. Actually, I wasn't stuck--I had hung up on an old chunk of a log that I didn't see in the tall grass. I centered over it with my tractor so that my wheels couldn't get any traction so I couldn't pull off of it. I was high and dry, in a manner of speaking. Larry pulled me backward and got me clear.

I was bush hogging without my sunglasses, which was a bad thing, but at least the brim of my cap helped a little by keeping the glare from shining directly into my eyes. So, naturally, a tree limb knocked the cap off of my head, it fell off the back of the tractor and I ran over it with the bush hog. Yep, I bush hogged my own cap. It was no longer recognizable as an actual cap and was therefore useless as a shield for my eyes. Oh, well, such is life for a boy named Roy.

But it was still Monday and I was still bush hogging, so things could have gotten worse--and they did. On one of my rounds, I ran over a really, really dried-out cow patty. Of course, I had run over millions of cow patties before with a bush hog, so it was pretty much a routine matter. But this was a Monday. A Monday with a curse on it.

That cow patty was instantly pulverized and, for some reason, was thrown high into the air so I was showered with itsy-bitsy, teeny-weeny particles of dried out cow patty.

Ordinarily, you might think it was bad ENOUGH to get showered with a cow patty. But, no, not for good old Roy. It just so happens that I occasionally take a soda pop with me when I go to the pasture. I keep it in the tool box on the wheel well by my seat so I can have a sip or two once in a while. Well, when I got my cow patty shower was one of those times when I was just getting ready to take a slug from my soda. I had the lid off and a few cow patty particles fell right into the soda pop. I really hated that. I'm not ordinarily a wasteful person but I poured out the rest of my soda and threw the bottle into the dumpster. You have to draw the line somewhere. Know what I mean?

Well, Monday was just about over and done with and I tried not to push my luck by doing anything extraordinary. Warmed up a few leftovers for supper. Didn't try to go to town for regular milk. Didn't try to operate any machinery with too many moving parts.

According to the calendar, the next day was supposed to be a Tuesday. I hoped it was not a Tuesday with an identity crisis that thought it was a Monday.

Chapter 37

Come 'n get it

When I got home at about 5:10 on 8 January 2008, the house was dark. No, I'm not talking about its mental attitude or its outlook on life. I mean, it was physically dark. The electricity was off. The next day, I learned that a tree had fallen across the power lines between home and town but at the moment, I was in the dark. Not only that, but I couldn't see, either.

Since I didn't know why the power was off, it was reasonable to speculate that it might be off for a long time and I might as well get on with the business at hand. It was cold, so the first priority was to build a fire in my wood-burning heating stove. In the back of my mind was the thought that I could warm a little supper on top of the stove, since I couldn't use the kitchen stove, which was electric.

I had a flashlight, so I used it to light my way as I proceeded to feed newspaper and kindling into the living room stove. Somewhere during that process, I turned off the flashlight and laid it down somewhere. I had needed it to accumulate the fire starting materials but I didn't need it to put them into the stove.

When I got ready to light the fire, I couldn't find the matches. So, I looked for the flashlight. I couldn't find that, either. What was the deal? It was a small house and I live alone. How difficult could it be to find something? I was the last person to touch it. After feeling over everything in the house, I did find the flashlight. With a source of light, I didn't have to use my sense of touch to find the matches but it still took longer than I thought it should have.

Before I started the fire, I put the flashlight in the pocket of my field jacket--I certainly was not about to lay it down, again. While the fire was getting cranked up, I fed some larger pieces of wood into the stove. I needed to get a larger fire going in order to warm up my supper.

I removed my jacket and rolled up my sleeves to wash my hands so I could work with the food. I knew there wasn't much in the refrigerator but I had some previously cooked lima beans. All I had to do was put some of them into a pie pan, add a little margarine, put the pan on the stove and wait.

I preferred to have light for the food preparation process, so I went to get the flashlight out of my jacket pocket. I couldn't remember where I had put the jacket. I assumed it was in the living room because that's where I was when I decided to take it off. Again, there I was again, feeling of everything in the house, looking for my jacket. I finally found it hanging on the back of a chair in the kitchen. I must have been wandering about while I was in the process of taking it off.

Finally, I got my beans ladled into a pie pan and set it on the stove. That's when I had an idea that some biscuits would go really well with the beans. I realized I could not cook them in the kitchen stove so I figured I would nuke them in the microwave. They would come out flat but they would be edible.

I popped open a can of biscuits, put them on a microwaveable plate and started to put them into the microwave. That's when I realized that, if the electric stove wouldn't work, then the electric microwave wouldn't work, either. However, all was not lost. I found another metal pie pan, transferred the biscuits to it and put it on the stove in the living room along with the lima beans.

After I stoked the fire again, I knew it would be awhile before everything would be ready, so I decided to have a shower while supper was cooking. Although the water heater was electric, I knew that I would have enough water for the shower. That's the first part of the evening that went as planned. I didn't run out of hot water. Will wonders never cease?

And I did not lose the flashlight while I was in the shower. I had laid a towel on the sink right in front of the shower door and I had put the flashlight on top of the towel. However, while I was in the shower, my poor old brain forgot that the flashlight was on the towel so, when I reached out for the towel and shook it out, I knocked the flashlight to the floor, where it promptly fell to pieces. By the time I had groped around and gathered up the various pieces of the flashlight, I didn't need the towel. I had air-dried.

So I got dressed and went back to the living room to check on supper. In the process of feeding a few more sticks of wood into the stove, I struck the corner of the stove with a chunk of wood. This jarred the stove, which caused some soot to fall off of the stovepipe right into the beans. Luckily, they were large lima beans (commonly called butter beans). Therefore, they were reasonably light colored. That made it a little easier to find most of the soot flakes. Under the beam of my newly assembled flashlight, the soot showed up very well against the color of the beans and bean soup. I reflected that it was a good thing I wasn't warming up pinto beans (commonly called brown beans). The flakes of soot would have blended in quite well with the pinto beans, making them difficult to find. Thank goodness for small favors.

The biscuits were another matter. It was a fairly easy task to find the soot that had landed on the bread. But the biscuits were still quite doughy, so it was almost impossible to separate the flakes from the dough. This precipitated another search. I had never put the flashlight down again (after I had reassembled it) so I was able to use it to search the house for a pair of tweezers, with which I picked most of the soot off of the biscuits.

It may have been my imagination but it seemed to take pert' near forever for the beans to get warm enough to eat. That was a mystery. The fire was burning really well. The stove was metal. The pie pan was metal and it was in direct contact with the metal stove. There should have been plenty of heat being transferred to the beans. It was happening but it certainly wasn't happening very quickly.

Eventually, the beans did get warm enough to eat, although the biscuits never made a transformation from their original doughy mass. Luckily, I had a package of crackers, which would serve as substitute bread. I'm a pure bred original country boy--I just can't eat without bread. I have to have a spoon or fork in one hand and a chunk of bread in the other (or at least, some sort of pseudo-bread). It's the law of the land.

I set up my computer desk as a supper table. I used a piece of tape to hang my flash- light from the overhead shelf so it would shine down on my eating area. I wouldn't have been able to use my kitchen table because it didn't have anything overhead from which to hang my flashlight.

Anyway, after all the aggravation and preparation, I had my pan of beans, my crackers and a glass of strawberry kool-aid. I was finally ready to enjoy my supper. I stirred my beans as well as I could. They had never really got hot enough to completely melt the butter but I decided to cut my losses. I'd had a rough day and I figured I was one of the lucky ones in the neighborhood. At least, I had something to eat, such as it was.

I settled down in front of my makeshift dining area, scooted my chair up to my "table", grabbed a cracker and dipped a spoonful of beans. It was exactly 7:15 pm. It had taken two hours to reach this objective but I felt SO victorious.

Just as I put the first hard-earned spoonful of food into my mouth, the lights came on.

P.S. Are lima beans supposed to crunch when you chew them?

Chapter 38

Not for Wimps

"Help, I've fallen and I can't get up". These are the words that ran through my mind at about 3:05 pm on Sunday, 24 April 2011. And truer words were never spoken. A heavy rain had started just a few minutes before. In the midst of the deluge, I was rushing across a wet patch of ground with both hands loaded with bags of groceries.

Just as I was crossing a particularly muddy spot, my right knee went out on me, as it has been known to do from time to time over the past few years. I can usually catch my balance with my other leg but this time, the ground was just too slippery. My forward momentum sent me sprawling headlong to the ground.

As groceries went flying in every direction, I made a perfect one-point landing on the front of my right shoulder. The pain was overwhelming. I thrashed about on the ground for awhile. Every part of my body that was facing downward was getting covered in mud and every part that was facing upward was getting soaked by the downpour.

I squirmed around, trying to find a way to get back to my feet. I could do absolutely nothing with my right arm and, if not for the agony in my right shoulder, I would have been hard-pressed to convince myself that it was still attached to my body.

I couldn't roll anywhere for two reasons: 1-the act of rolling would require at least a miniscule amount of assistance from my right arm and that was totally outside the realm of possibilities. 2-the act of rolling would put pressure on that right shoulder and that was something that I was going to avoid, at all costs.

I somehow managed to inchworm my way over to my truck. With my left arm, I was able to use various parts of the truck to drag my body into a vertical position. Slowly and painfully, I gathered my groceries, one at a time and dropped them into the floorboard on the passenger's side of the truck. Then I climbed behind the wheel. Or rather, I wiggled into the truck on the driver's side. My efforts were not pretty. I wished I had a movie camera. I would have won the competition on "America's Funniest Home Videos".

I reached over and got the truck started with my left hand. No problem.

My truck has a five speed manual transmission with the gear shift lever mounted on the floor. Problem. The truck was already in first gear and was pointed toward the road. Problem solved.

I took off and picked up enough speed to shift into second gear. Problem. I held the steering wheel in generally the right direction with my knees while I reached over with my left hand to shift gears. Problem solved.

This procedure worked equally well for third and fourth gear--I wouldn't need to shift into fifth gear because it is for speeds over 50 mph--sort of like overdrive. At the time, I was still on a gravel road where the top manageable speed is about 40 mph, even for an able-bodied driver.

During this entire process, my right arm hung uselessly off the side of my body and my right hand, equally useless, was lying on the seat beside me. My poor shoulder was sending some very vivid messages of pain and agony to my brain for every pothole I hit, for every rut I jumped, indeed, for every pebble that crossed my path.

Luckily, I made it home without too many mishaps…and without killing anybody, which is a good thing. Getting out of the truck presented only one problem-I did not know how much it was going to hurt to change the position of my hand because that changed the stress points on my shoulder. Having my arm hang uselessly at my side did not guarantee that the pain was going to remain constant. As it turned out, there was absolutely nothing I could do with the right side of my upper body. It was just impossible to move my hand. I found an astonishing number of tasks to be beyond my ability. Tasks which I had come to accept as "givens" I couldn't pick up a biscuit or a glass of soda pop.

I couldn't reach out for a doorknob or a light switch. I realized that being injured was going to turn out to be, not only painful, but darned inconvenient, as well.

Taking a shower was somewhat of an adventure. Rather, an adventure in comic entertainment. It hurt to have the water hit my shoulder and run off my arm but still, some of my efforts could have been funny, even to me. For example, how do you wash your right ear with your left hand-unless you are a contortionist, which I am not? How do you wash your left arm if your right hand is useless?

Trying to get into bed was another adventure. Simply drawing back the covers was very awkward with just one usable arm. Finding a comfortable position in which to sleep was also challenging because I usually sleep in the prone position. Well, yeah, I mean I'm usually prone while I am asleep, although I have been known to sleep quite soundly while sitting up watching television, while sitting up driving, while sitting up listening to longwinded sermons in church. Anyway, where was I? Oh yeah, regarding comfortable sleeping positions... well, I hardly ever sleep flat on my back. No, I don't know why I don't, I just don't. That's another one of the many mysteries in my life that I'll never figure out. Anyway, lying on my right side was out because my shoulder couldn't take the weight of my body on it. However, lying on my left side was also out because my shoulder couldn't take the weight of my right arm hanging off of it, even though my elbow would support some of the weight against the mattress. Lying on my stomach was out because I rarely ever sleep on my stomach. No, again, I don't know why I don't, I just don't. Chalk it up as another one of my life's mysteries. Besides, it reminded my of the pain I had experienced while I was laid out flat on my stomach in the mud.

On Monday morning, I decided that I couldn't put up with the pain any longer so I called the VA hospital outpatient clinic in Russellville. Why did I choose the VA instead of just going to the emergency room at Saint Mary's, you may ask. Well, for one thing, I am a veteran so I am entitled to receive treatment at a VA hospital, with an appropriate co-pay, of course. Besides, I'm extremely poor so a visit to a regular hospital emergency room would put me in debt for the rest of my natural born days because I wouldn't get away with just a co-pay.

So, there I was, on the phone with the VA. They told me they couldn't see me until Wednesday afternoon. That meant another two and one-third days of pain. Fifty-six hours of pain. Three thousand three hundred and sixty minutes of pain.

On Wednesday, Robert drove me to Russellville for my appointment. When the doctor saw my condition, he said I should have come in on Monday. I didn't bother to remind him that I was following doctor's orders by waiting until Wednesday. He thought my shoulder looked so bad, he decided to send me to Little Rock so the main hospital could do x-rays and a CT scan. In fact, he wanted me to go immediately. At the time, it was already 4:00 pm, but I agreed with him and told him I would go.

I already knew Robert wouldn't be able to take me to Little Rock. His tires (not to mention the rest of his car) would not survive the trip. I also knew that my truck would not make it, either. So, I went to Plan B and called Shirley. I knew she would move Heaven and Earth to get me down there.

Okay, I have to admit this. Calling Shirley is never Plan B. She is, has always been, and will always be Plan A. Naturally, she agreed to take me. By the time the doctor had made the various calls to arrange for my treatment after normal hours, Shirley and Dennis were ready to depart. The trip was uneventful. We were going INTO Little Rock while everybody and his uncle were trying to get OUT of the city, so we just about constituted a one-car traffic jam, except we weren't jammed.

The x-rays were taken first while we waited for a CT technician to arrive. Everybody had already gone home at the end of their work day, so a tech came in to work overtime just for me. The final analysis was 'torn ligaments and damage to the rotator cuff.

They gave me some drugs and showed me how to adjust the sling that I was going to be wearing. All of the various doctors that had got involved were pretty sure that they were going to have to operate. I was dead-set against that, and I told them so. They did not agree to cancel that option but they did agree to postpone it until they could see how I progressed with my arm immobilized. I'm not actually afraid of being operated on--I've been operated on a few times before, for various wounds, injuries and damage to my body and the final outcome has never been quite as successful as anticipated--so I wanted to be the one who decided to go ahead with it, if it proved to be inevitable.

I'm mostly retired, although I do have a part-time job gathering eggs. Luckily, we were between chicken batches when I took my fall, so I just took a vacation for about a month. Not having to do very much work was alright but I couldn't really enjoy my vacation because I couldn't do a lot of anything else, either, although I did a lot of weird exercises to regain enough mobility so that the operation option would not be required. That effort, at least, was successful. Operating was not an absolute "must".

I got to the point where I could do quite a bit with my right arm, as long as I kept my arm low. I couldn't reach upward or forward. Or to the side, either. It was frustrating, to say the least. It took four months before I could reach out with my right hand to take my sunglasses off the dashboard of my truck.

Then, I fell again. On 24 October 2011. Six months, to the day (almost to the hour) after I had fallen and injured my right shoulder, I fell again and injured my left shoulder. I took a nosedive off the steps of my porch and landed on my left side.

It was de ja vu all over again. Shirley and Dennis took me back to the VA hospital in Little Rock. As before, we spent most of the evening waiting for the results of the x-rays. Although the diagnosis wasn't quite as bad, this time. Torn ligaments in my shoulder but no serious damage to my rotator cuff.

Another vacation. A mini-vacation, this time. Arm in a sling, but only for a few days. The black and blue marks were mostly gone in just over a week (instead of a month). Yes, it was rough being physically handicapped but I had been in similar situations on several occasions, before, so I knew I could tough it out. The thing was, I always knew those times were temporary. That always makes almost anything easier to accept. I can't even begin to comprehend how a person would be able to cope with a handicap that is known to be permanent. I don't know how I could live, even IF I could live, if I knew I would never regain the use of an injured part of my body. Or perhaps that a part of my body might be missing. I have a deep and abiding respect for truly disabled people who are PERMANENTLY handicapped. They have to be truly mentally tough.

I'm glad of one thing. At least, I waited until I had a reasonable amount of healing to my right arm before I disabled my left arm. So it was one of those good news/bad news situations. Even in my un-lucky-ness, I'm still a pretty lucky guy. If I was a younger man, I would have made a much more rapid recovery from injuries like these, but even though I'm now rather ancient, I still have a reasonably tough disposition, which is a good thing because, as Shirley says, "Old age is not for wimps".

Thicker Than Water

Roy Morris

Random Observations

Chapter 39

Time

I use a wood-burning stove to heat my house (and have been doing so for years). Now you're asking the question, "What in the world does that have to do with time?". I'm glad you asked because I'm going to tell you. In fact, if you keep reading, I was going to tell you, anyway, whether you had asked or not.

You see, it takes time to use a wood-burning stove. First, you have to wad up the old newspapers or whatever you're going to use to start the fire in the stove. Second, you add some kindling. Third, you put a few larger sticks of reasonably seasoned (dried) wood on top of that. Fourth, you add at least a couple of sticks of green (fresh cut) wood to "hold" the fire. Fifth, you keep adding green wood every couple of hours for as long as you want to keep warm, even if you have to get out of bed to feed the stove. For me, there is a sixth step--well, it isn't actually a step but it is a predicament that complicates my daily routine. You see, I live alone. So there is no one there to keep the fire going throughout the day. Every evening when I get home from work, I have to restart the fire because it will have burned out in my absence. So I have to go through the required steps more often than many other people who use wood to heat with.

All of these steps take time. And the sad part is that those five steps to the art of getting warm (and staying that way) are only a small part of the entire process of heating a house with a wood burning stove.

You have to go out into the woods, select a tree that will serve as firewood, cut down the tree (preferably with a chain saw, although I've cut down many a tree with either an ax or a two man crosscut saw), cut the trunk and most of the limbs in chunks (usually somewhere between ten inches to twenty inches long, depending on the size of the stove or fireplace), split these chunks and the larger limbs into pieces that will fit through the door of the stove, put the left over smallest branches into a pile to be burned in place later so that wind or cattle won't scatter them all over the area, load the stove-size pieces onto a truck or a tractor-drawn trailer (in my day, it was a horse-drawn trailer), haul the wood to the vicinity of the house, put it into a woodpile or stack it onto the porch so you won't have far to go when it's time to throw a stick or two into the stove.

In case it hasn't occurred to you, I might mention that you need to own the land where you are going to cut wood, or you need to have an arrangement with the people who do own the land. You may also have noticed that an essential part of this wood-gathering process is the possession of either a truck or a trailer (and a tractor with which to pull it).

If you don't own any of these things, or if you don't have a friend or relative who owns equipment that you can borrow, then you will have to pay someone to cut and deliver firewood for you. That wouldn't make much sense to me. If I'm going to actually PAY somebody to furnish me with firewood, then I might just as well be paying somebody to bring propane or butane, or whatever, and put it into a tank or bottle out by the side of the house, and not even bother with using wood, in the first place.

Let's not forget about the kindling. A lot of people might prefer small slivers of cedar or pine but just about any small pieces of wood will suffice, as long as they are well dried out. I use just about anything that I might pick up from along fencerows or under trees. The point is that you do need this stuff and it's going to take time to collect it.

And, of course, when you burn wood, there will be some residue… ashes. After a couple of days (even sooner if it's really cold and you're burning a lot of wood), you will have to scoop the ashes out of the stove and dump them outside. You will need a small metal shovel of some type. Likewise, you'll need some sort of metal receptacle, like a bucket, in which to carry the ashes. Furthermore, you'll need a pair of leather gloves to protect your hands. The ashes will be throwing off a lot of heat and your hand will be only a couple of inches above them while you're holding the handle of that bucket. And remember, the scooping and carrying of those ashes is going to take time.

Now, where are you going to dump the ashes? You realize you can't throw them just anywhere. You need to put them where they won't start a brush fire. And, for the sake of appearances, you must consider the fact that, after a period of time, you're going to have a big pile of ashes somewhere outside near the house.

Speaking of appearances, those ashes aren't the only residue that results from wood burning. There will be smoke and soot and it isn't all going to fly up the chimney. Every piece of furniture, every surface, every object in the house is going to collect a layer of ugly looking black soot. It's going to take a lot of time to clean the house…and you're going to have to clean it a lot more often than you would if you weren't using a wood burning stove.

So, let's review what is going to be required in order to use a wood-burning stove. First, of course, you need a stove. That doesn't qualify as an extra expense because you will need some sort of heating device, anyway, whether it operates on butane, electricity, kerosene or wood. However, everything else you will need qualifies as an extra expense because, if you weren't burning wood, you wouldn't need these things. For instance, the land where you will cut the wood and the kindling. Whether you own it, lease it, or just have permission to go there, it still has to exist. You will have to own or borrow a truck or a tractor/trailer combination. You will need a chain saw, crosscut saw or ax to fell a tree and to cut it into stove size chunks. Some other necessary possessions would be a mawl, a splitting wedge or an ax to split the chunks so they will fit through the door of the stove. You'll need a metal shovel, metal bucket and a pair of thick gloves in order to handle the ash residue. And you might as well add in the fact that you will need extra spray cleaner and paper towels to use in the process of cleaning the soot off of all your furniture.

The simple life isn't as simple as it seems, is it? I don't get paid for cutting, hauling or splitting my own wood, or for carrying out the ashes or for cleaning the house. What would I charge myself? I couldn't afford to pay me what all that would actually be worth.

So all of the time I spend doing that stuff comes out of my so-called free time. That's time I could have spent doing other stuff, like visiting with family and friends, doing the regular chores around the house, bowling, shopping, reading…or perhaps, just writing stories about how I spend my time.

Chapter 40

Magic Gas Container

I have a gas container that just keeps growing. But it grows only on the inside. It doesn't actually LOOK any larger on the outside. Maybe it's a magic gas container. Maybe the outside of it exists only in this dimension while the inside exists in another dimension. A dimension where space is larger than it looks. Maybe it's a trick that they do with mirrors. Or maybe the inside of my gas container has some sort of secret compression device that makes liquids smaller in volume.

I can't think of any other explanation for it. It wasn't all that long ago that the inside of that gas container would only hold three dollars' worth of gas. After a short period of time, it would hold seven dollars worth. Just a few days ago, it held nine dollars' worth. This morning, the inside of that gas container held eleven dollars' worth of gas. But the container still doesn't look any larger on the outside. That just has to be magic.

Chapter 41

It's About Time

How many 'times' are there?
Making time…does that mean we can manufacture an hour?
Doing time, in prison
Tea time…if you're British
Double time….a slow jog in the military
Break time at work
Lunch time
Dinner time
Full time…a regular employee
Part time…an irregular employee
Quality time with your kids
Waste time on the street corner
Take your own sweet time
Kill time while you're waiting for a doctor appointment
Tell time with a watch
Spend time with your friends
Have a hot time in the old town tonight
A good time was had by all
Hey, kids, what time is it?
It's Howdy Doody Time
Read Time magazine
Do things in a timely manner
If I could save time in a bottle….a Jim Croce song

A timing device at hot rod races
Find the time to take care of something
Tax time
Miller time
Nap time
Beddie-bye time
Time is money
Time lock safes
Some beauty is timeless
Travel through time
Kids learn the times tables
Time in
Time out
Right on time
Time share condos
When we build some buildings, we put a time capsule in the
     cornerstone
If I were about to die, could I swallow one of those time capsules
     and live longer?
After all, some medicines have time release capsules

Chapter 42

I'm so ugly

I'm so ugly, I have to sneak up on a mirror.

I'm so ugly, hound dogs won't identify with me.

I'm so ugly, my imaginary friends won't play with me.

I'm so ugly, my younger brothers are lucky to be alive.

I'm so ugly, at Halloween, I don't have to wear a mask.

I'm so ugly, I'm listed among America's Least Wanted.

I'm so ugly, I could be the poster child for birth control pills.

I'm so ugly, my driver's license picture actually makes me look good.

I'm so ugly, my last girlfriend referred to me as her insignificant other.

I'm so ugly, when I was born, the doctor didn't know which end to slap.

I'm so ugly, nobody would take me at face value. My face doesn't have any value.

I'm so ugly, my parents tied a pork chop around my neck so the dog would play with me.

He buried it while I was still attached.

I'm so ugly, I decided God must have a sense of humor. Take a look at this face. Does this look like the work of a serious artist?

I'm so ugly, when I was a teenager, I took a girl parking at the lake to "watch the sub-marine races" and she actually expected to see submarines.

I'm so ugly, I had no choice but to become a comedian. Every time I asked some girl for a date, she would look at me with a puzzled expression for a minute, then she would smile and say, "You're a comedian, aren't you?"

I'm so ugly, when our mother once took us kids for a train ride, and the conductor came through checking tickets, he said to my mother, "Ma'am, it's okay for you and your children to ride up here in coach, but your pet monkey is going to have to ride in the baggage car".

I'm so ugly, I have decided to stop calling myself ugly. I have registered myself with the federal government as being appearance impaired. Now, if some girl refuses to go out with me, I can take her to court for discrimination against the handicapped. After all, a court-ordered date is better than no date, at all.

I'm so ugly, even my shadow doesn't want to be associated with me. In fact, this is my sixteenth shadow. The first four just would not do what I wanted them to do. I had no choice but to fire them. Two shadows sneaked away while I was in the dark. When I came back out in the light, they didn't come back out with me. Four other shadows joined the federal witness protection program and changed their identities. And do you know how difficult it is to find left handed shadows? Only one in twelve is left handed, you know. I tried working with a few right handed shadows but I was getting very confused. I tried walking backwards. That didn't help. Besides, I kept bumping into things. And do you think any of those right handed shadows warned me? Nope. One shadow I had for about two months just wasn't working out at all because it was a female shadow. I had a lot of trouble with that one. It was very embarrassing just trying to change clothes. I had to take showers with the lights off. And it was making me walk funny. You see, I don't usually swish my hips. I was sending the wrong message to society whenever my female shadow and I were out in public. I received six indecent proposals--

and four of them were from men. And the female shadow started trying to dictate what we would do…a couple of times, I caught myself putting on makeup. I decided I had to end our relationship before my female shadow had me wearing women's clothing and high heels. I wouldn't be able to live like that.

An ugly rich man is a rich man but an ugly poor man is an ugly poor man.

Thicker Than Water

Roy Morris

My Humble Opinion

Chapter 43

Hazing in the Marine Corps

I want to break away from my usual type of stories about derring-do and mishaps to say something about hazing because, along about this period of time (February 1997) in the sequence of events, the Commandant of the Marine Corps, General Krulak, appeared on television and talked about it. I simply had to make a statement about this.

I promised myself that I wouldn't actually try to defend the practice of hazing, itself, as some forms of hazing are particularly heinous and despicable. But I want to explain enough so that those of you who are not Marines, former Marines or part of the Marine family might have some inkling of understanding regarding this particular type of hazing. There are many mottos, slogans and sayings which describe or pertain to the Marine Corps and I'll cover a few of them to build a base of background information for you.

'Semper Fidelis', as it is roughly translated, means Always Faithful. The unspoken remainder of that motto is…to God, Country and Corps. As Marines, the priorities of our chosen profession are established in that order. We usually say 'Semper Fi'.

'Gung Ho' became a popular Marine motto/saying after Lieutenant Colonel Carlson became Commanding Officer of a Marine Raider Battalion (newly formed) in 1942. The President's son was the Executive Officer. Carlson had a very extensive military back-ground, having even served, at one time, with the Chinese Communist

Route Army. The term Gung Ho is Chinese and some people think it means "pull together" but it is more correctly translated as "Strive for Harmony".

'First to Fight' is a line right out of the Marine Corps Hymn, which is 'First to fight for right and freedom and to keep our honor clean'. It doesn't mean that some Marine is the first to pick a fight with some drunk in a bar. It simply illustrates that, for more than two and a quarter centuries, the Marine Corps has been the favorite choice, a Force in Readiness, whenever military intervention was required to quell an insurrection, to reverse a hostile takeover, to subdue an evil dictator, to right a wrong.

The Few-The Proud-The Marines. This phrase illustrates our status as the smallest (numerically speaking) of the US military forces. We don't want a lot of recruits...only the best. There is only one period in US history when the Marine Corps accepted draftees, and even then, they were kicked out if they did not pass muster in boot camp. We don't want just anybody. Our standards are high. We aren't like the army--we don't join you, you join us. You have to WANT to be a Marine. And you have to EARN the right to wear the Marine Corps emblem.

'Retreat, hell. We just got here'. This statement was made by a Marine Commander, just arrived at a Korean battle area, after having been told by an Army officer they would have to evacuate.

'The Marines have landed and the situation is well in hand'. This is a quote by an Army officer on a hostile beachfront, who was greatly relieved after Marines hit the beach and joined the battle.

'Uncommon valor was a common virtue'. This is another quote by an officer of one of our sister services after he had witnessed countless acts of bravery and courage by Marines on the battlefield.

'We don't promise you a rose garden'. This was a recruiting slogan from the early 1960's. The message was clear. If you think you're tough enough, you're welcome to try to earn a Marine Corps Emblem but we certainly won't make it easy for anyone to win our Eagle, Globe and Anchor. Wearing our emblem is a very special privilege, accorded to very few. It's an honor that we guard carefully.

'Once a Marine, always a Marine'. That statement illustrates our dedication to the Corps. We may take off the uniform but we'll never take off the mind-set, the ideals or the attitudes that make being a Marine something so very special.

There are many other sayings. Fellow members of the Band of Brothers who read this will wonder how I skipped one or two of their favorites. But hopefully, by now, you're starting to get an insight into the type of person it takes to be a Marine. In some way or another, each Marine is one of a kind. He's not your average guy. Generically speaking, of course. I'm not forgetting that there have been many notable women who have earned the Emblem.

Now, about this hazing business. As if the honor and prestige of being a Marine isn't enough, already, there are elites within the elite. Scout/Snipers. Force Reconnaissance. Drill Instructors. Close Combat Instructors (hand to hand unarmed combat). Primary Marksmanship Instructors. Pilots. Parachutists. Platoon Commanders. You know how the saying goes: Best of the Best.

Now, regarding the hazing incident of which the Commandant was referring: The device, called "jump wings", which signifies successful completion of parachute training is an emblem which has two stick pins, by which it is attached to the shirt just above a Marine's personal ribbons and decorations. The stick pins are pushed through the fabric of the shirt or blouse, then fasteners are attached to the stick pins on the inside of the shirt to hold it in place. After a trainee makes ten successful jumps in training, the instructor sticks the jump wings onto the trainee's shirt and pounds it with his fist. Without the clasp fasteners on the back of the stick pins, the stick pins break the skin of the trainee's chest, causing blood to flow. That's the way Marine jump wings have been "pinned on", virtually since parachute training was added to the Marine training syllabus in the 1940's. The same procedure applies to the "pinning on" ceremony when a Marine earns the device which indicates he has successfully completed SCUBA training (Self Contained Underwater Breathing Apparatus)

Every Marine is familiar with these practices, from the lowest private all the way up the chain of command. It's common knowledge. I don't imagine any of us ever thought there was a so-called "code of silence" about it. I'm sure it would never have occurred to anybody that it was a big secret.

When the Commandant of the Marine Corps appeared on the Today Show in February 1997, he expressed shock and surprise that such a procedure was being practiced within our ranks. He promised that the individuals involved would be discovered, investigated and disciplined.

Since he was, by inference, indicating that he was unaware of this, I suppose the phrase "plausible deniability" would be appropriate. To this, I can only say, "No comment". Sorry, General.

When a Private (E-1) gets promoted to Private First Class (E-2), he puts a stripe on the sleeve of his uniform shirt. Every succeeding promotion in the enlisted ranks, through either Master Gunnery Sergeant (E-9) or Sergeant Major (E-9), brings a change in the appearance of his chevrons (his insignia of rank).

With every promotion comes a ceremony called "Pinning on the Stripes", in which every Marine in the platoon who already outranks the new promotee forms a double line in the barracks or on the parade ground. The promotee must walk through that gauntlet, having his arms punched by all those Marines who outrank him. I have seen Marines whose arms were black and blue from the shoulder to the elbow.

The three lowest enlisted ranks (Private, Private First Class, Lance Corporal) are called non-rates. Corporals and Sergeants are known as noncommissioned officers (NCO's). Staff Sergeants, Gunnery Sergeants, Master Sergeants (or First Sergeants) and Master Gunnery Sergeants (or Sergeants Major) are known as staff noncommissioned officers (Staff NCO's).

Because of the courage, ferocity and daring displayed by NCO's in previous battles--and because so many of them lost their lives--all Marine NCO's are privileged to wear a red (blood) stripe on the seams of their trousers to signify the blood that was shed by their brother Marine NCO's. So when a young Marine gets promoted to Corporal, he will get his arms punched and his legs kicked. Yes, those NCO blood stripes get pinned on, too.

But we aren't hazing these people. We're honoring them. We want to pin their stripes on so hard, they will never come off. By punching or kicking the promotee, we are thusly expressing a sincere hope that he will never do anything to bring dishonor or disgrace to his rank, thereby losing those hard-earned stripes.

It is a rite of passage, a form of initiation. You should ask me, sometime, about the ceremony aboard a ship when a Marine crosses the equator for the first time...then again, maybe you shouldn't.

Yes, I am a former Marine. My enlisted ranks were: Private (E-1). Private First Class (E-2). Lance Corporal (E-3). Corporal (E-4).

Sergeant (E-5). Staff Sergeant (E-6). Gunnery Sergeant (E-7). My officer ranks were: Warrant Officer (W-1). Chief Warrant Officer (W-2). My assignments were many and diverse, but the most notable were these: Viet-Nam, twice. Fire Team Leader. Squad Leader. Platoon Sergeant. Close Combat Instructor (Shorin-Ryu Karate). Primary Marksmanship Instructor (Rifle and Pistol). Company Physical Training Officer. Platoon Commander.

Once a Marine, always a Marine. Semper Fi. Gung Ho. OOOO-RAH!!

Chapter 44

Bullies

I don't like bullies. This attitude is not a recent development. I have never liked them. I started having trouble with bullies in grade school because I was a small kid. Actually, I stayed pretty small--I was never taller than 5'7". But I did gain some weight. When I was 15, one of Dad's co-workers said I was built like a little Tarzan. And I was solid as a rock. There was no fat anywhere on me. But I was still short so I didn't LOOK big. By the time I was 18, I was 179 pounds with a 29 inch waist line.

Anyway, I've told you that in order to tell you this. In the process of getting to be the way I eventually was, I spent a lot of time dealing with bullies in school. I was 16 when I had my last confrontation with a bully, at least on my behalf. I had a few confrontations with bullies, later on, on behalf of some smaller, weaker kids. I would stick up for anybody who was too small or too scared to stick up for themselves and the school bullies eventually learned to mind their manners while I was in the area.

My final confrontation, on my own behalf, occurred in the school hallway. One of the bullies came up behind me and poked me in the butt. When I turned around, he held up his fist with his middle finger extended and said, with a smirk, "Looks to me like you're a quart low".

With one hand, I grabbed him by the neck, picked him up and held him against the wall with his feet dangling a foot off the floor. He grabbed my wrist with both hands but couldn't get free. By the time he stopped struggling, some of the other students realized he was in serious trouble. It took three burly football players to drag him away from the wall and pry my hand away from his neck. It was his good fortune that I had grabbed him with my right arm, my weak arm.

While he laid on the floor, retching, coughing and gasping, I looked down at him and said, "If you ever touch me again, if you even brush against me, there won't be enough football players in this school to save you. Do you understand?"

He couldn't speak very loudly but he nodded his head and whispered, "Yes, sir". From that day on, he wouldn't come near me. He would go out one door and walk all the way around the building and come back in through another door, if necessary, to avoid passing me in the hallway.

By today's standards, I could have been charged with terroristic threatening. Or even assault. Maybe even attempted murder. By my standards, I was simply correcting the actions of a bully and a jerk. I have no patience with somebody like that and I honestly believe that a person like that doesn't deserve any consideration.

If he had simply pushed or nudged me, his life might not have been in danger. But he touched me in a place where a normal male would never touch another male and I was willing to face the consequences for making him pay the full penalty for his transgression.

I suppose he might have eventually worked up enough nerve to have some of his friends gang up on me but no matter what damage was inflicted on me, he knew that if I survived, then he would never feel safe again…for the rest of his life.

I don't know if his life may have flashed before his eyes while I had him in my power but if it did, he probably didn't like what he saw regarding his final destination.

Chapter 45

Chosen by God

During Bible study on 1 Aug 2007, I turned the other cheek. That was not something that I had a lot of experience at and I did not enjoy it. After I learned that Saul had been a very active persecutor of Christians and had killed many of them, then changed his name to Paul when he became a Christian convert, himself, after a night of great personal revelations, I thought of him as a hypocrite and decided I didn't like him, especially after reading some of his writings. During Bible study, I made the mistake of saying that I didn't really like Paul very much and questioning why he had changed a statement that Jesus had made--or, rather, he made a different statement on the same subject that Jesus had been talking about.

The minister took umbrage at what I had said about Paul, who happened to be one of the pastor's heroes. So, his statement to me was, "I'll say this in front of Brother Tim, and Brother Kevin and Brother Leon, but YOU don't need to be talking bad about Paul". At the time, he was pointing his finger at me. I can't truthfully say he shook his finger in my face because he was three pews away from me and his finger didn't actually shake but my impression was that he desperately WANTED to shake his finger in my face.

He completely disregarded the presence of the women who were at Bible study with us. It apparently did not occur to him that he was making the statement in front of them, too, not just in front of the men. He didn't even acknowledge that they were there. And he obviously felt that what he said was so important that he wanted to point out that it was being said in front of unimpeachable witnesses. Well, all of his named witnesses had their wives there--even the minister's wife was there--but presumably, none of them were important, at least, not important enough to be mentioned. The same sort of attitude that Paul had toward women.

But I was not "talking bad about Paul". True, I said that I did not particularly like him but that does not constitute talking bad about him. And the question that I asked was just a question and it did not mean I was "talking bad about Paul", either. So, the pastor's statement to me about "talking bad about Paul" was completely out of context with the conversation we were having, at the time.

And when he said, --YOU don't need to be talking bad about Paul", he put a lot of emphasis on the word, YOU. It seemed to me that he was really saying that there might actually be some people who would be qualified to talk bad about Paul, but I was most certainly not one of them. Even though I had heard him say that he, as our minister, could not and would not judge anybody, it certainly seemed as though he had judged me.

The problem with this situation is this: Several months previously, I had completed a reading of the entire New Testament and had quite a few questions, which I had written out in letter format and had given the letter to the pastor. In that letter, I had mentioned that Paul seemed to be a male chauvinist because of some statements he had written which were downgrading and demeaning toward women. The pastor had never answered any of the questions I had asked in my letter. In fact, he had never even approached me regarding those questions.

The statement he made to me at Bible study bothered me for a long time. I could not get it out of my mind. At the time, I passed it off as a joke, saying that I must have been serving as "Devil's Advocate" to liven up the Bible study. But the truth was, it had made me mad. In fact, it had made me furious. But I had turned the other cheek because I still had a lot of respect for our pastor. After all, he had been the man who had led me to the altar when I was saved and he was the minister who baptized me, afterward.

When I went to church on Sunday, 5 Aug 2007, I was still moody and quiet because I was still upset about being forced to turn the other cheek but I sat in my favorite spot in the back pew and tried to enjoy the fellowship

During the service that day, the pastor mentioned that one of the church members had recently completed a reading of the Bible. That is quite an accomplishment and was worthy of note. Therefore, his feat should have been mentioned in church so that the rest of the congregation could applaud his efforts. The pastor even pointed out that he had questions based on his readings.

I was proud and happy for him. But it did occur to me that I had also read the Bible and had asked questions based on my readings--and I had never even got an honorable mention in church. And, perhaps my questions were quite different from the questions that other church member asked. Maybe his questions were more easily answered.

During the service that day, the pastor also mentioned Paul, at length, pointing out that Paul had been chosen by God, as if that made Paul out to be an extraordinary person. At least, that was the impression I got by the tone of his voice and the expression on his face. But Paul was just an ordinary person, except that he changed his name from Saul to distance himself from the Christian-hating persecutor he had been previously.

Being "chosen by God" is not what the pastor seems to believe it to be. After all, just consider the following examples:

King David was chosen by God, but when he got the chance, he went after another man's wife. And then he arranged for that man's death because he wanted to keep her. Chosen by God.

Jonah was chosen by God, but he tried to leave the country to avoid the responsibility that God was giving him. Of course, he didn't make a successful getaway, as we know, but he had to be forced to do his duty. Chosen by God.

Samson was chosen by God, but he apparently wasn't very bright. Several times, he pretended to tell Delilah the secret of his strength, and every time, she tried to use that knowledge to destroy him. Every single time. It shouldn't have taken much intelligence to figure out that if he ever really told her his secret, then it would definitely bring about his downfall. But he eventually told her the real secret, anyway. How many hints did he need to keep his fool mouth shut? How stupid that seems to me. Chosen by God.

Joseph was chosen by God, but when he was named as Overseer for the distribution of the Pharaoh's crops, he misused and abused the authority of his position by giving grain (apparently a great deal of grain) to his brothers and secretly giving their money back to them--on more than one occasion. And he even used that deed against his brothers, to coerce them into doing what he wanted. The grain was not His to give away. He was only the Overseer for distribution of it. It belonged to the Pharaoh, so actually what he did was to steal from his boss in order to benefit his family. Nepotism in its truest form. In my final analysis, he was a thief. Chosen by God.

Moses was chosen by God to lead his people, but Moses tried to get out of it by giving FIVE different excuses to evade the task. He tried to be a shirker. Chosen by God.

Yes, Paul wrote 13 books of the New Testament, but really, he just wrote 13 letters to 13 different church groups. And they were short letters so I wouldn't even say he was a prolific writer. So he wasn't extraordinary, after all.

In my humble opinion, there has only been one person who was truly extraordinary in all these thousands of years, well, actually three people. Joseph, Mary and Jesus. Mary was chosen by God but she was very afraid and probably would not have accepted her situation, if she had been given a choice. Joseph was chosen by God to take Mary as his wife in spite of her condition but he would have turned down this responsibility if he had not been convinced to accept it by an Angel of the Lord. Jesus was obviously chosen by God, since He was God's Son, but even He asked if His burden could be lifted from Him.

The pastor had formed an unfavorable opinion of me because of the questions I asked after having read the Bible, or perhaps because I had the audacity to ask questions, in the first place. He made his opinion of me obvious by declining to answer, or even comment on, the questions I had asked. He reinforced that opinion by chastising me during Bible study. He further reinforced that opinion by praising that other church member who had finished reading the Bible, while ignoring the fact that I had also done so.

I felt that I had no choice but to resign from membership in the Sweet Home Free Will Baptist Church. We had a basic difference of opinion that was very important and could have been detrimental to our status--his as a mentor, mine as a student.

Then, I told him that I forgave him. He ignored that little bit of communication, also.

P. S. I did have one final thought. What if I had been *Chosen by God* to test the pastor's patience. Do you think he would have passed or failed?

Chapter 46

Politicians

I've always been confused by politics. I consider elections to be a curse on the American Way of Life. One of the many things I can't comprehend is this: A politician comes on tv and says I did this, this and this. Then his opponent comes on and says no, he didn't, he did that, that and that. Now, folks, I've never once claimed to be a rocket scientist but it doesn't take too many smarts for me to figure out that ONE of those fellers is telling us a bald-faced lie. And then they claim that the other one is running a negative campaign, whoever the other ' may be. I wish the term 'negative campaigning' meant that none of them were actually running, at all.

Doesn't the FCC have an ethics committee? Surely, it's against the law for those folks to come on tv and just tell us a bunch of flat-out lies about themselves or each other. How can a politician come on tv and say "I approved this ad" and not get into trouble if it's obvious that the ad is a pack of lies?

Maybe politicians are like professional wrestlers. Wrestlers can make it look like they are killing each other and never get charged with assault and battery. Maybe politicians do like wrestlers, you know, get together and practice on each other before they come on tv so they come out at the end looking like they both did the right thing.

Cigarettes aren't allowed to advertise on tv anymore because they're bad for us. The way I see it, politicians are a lot worse for us than cigarettes. Maybe we ought to bring back the cigarette ads and ban the politicians. And folks, I have never smoked in my entire life but I'd rather smoke a whole pack than shake hands with one politician.

When I was an officer in the Marine Corps, I met a few politicians and had dealings with a few more and I can tell you this: I have never known a politician yet who actually filled a worthwhile niche in society. Sure, every single one of you can probably name one that you know of who you think is a decent sort of person so I'll make a deal with you. If you feel strongly enough about the one that you like, then get in touch with me. If you can prove your case to me, then I'll pay for advertising space in my local newspaper for you to run a rebuttal. What could be more fair? But you will have to really prove your case without using negative advertising.

I don't mind telling you that I have no respect for politicians at any level. But I have developed my opinion over a very long period of time while receiving quite an education regarding politicians so I have come to my conclusions about them honestly. The reason I am discussing politicians in this book is because most of the decisions they have made over the years have had a significant impact on my life (partially in regard to where I have spent major portions of my life--for example, in foreign countries while in the military service) but mostly in regard to my financial status--for example, 99.9% of the ways in which they spend my tax dollars are ways that do not meet with my approval.

One of the following chapters in this book is actually a reprint of the original version of an article I wrote during the last presidential election process. The final condensed version, titled *Owe Me a Living*, was published in *The Courier* newspaper in Russellville on 29 Sept 2012. If you are the least bit interested in WHY I have such a low opinion of politicians, in general, you might find the next few chapters to be very enlightening.

Chapter 47

Promises

On 28 March 2011, President Obama made a speech on television regarding Libya and Moammar Gaddafi. During the speech, he made the following promises:

We will do what we said we would do.

We will protect the interests of the people of the United States

We will look out for the welfare of our fellow human beings.

That's all well and good. We (the people of the United States) value the concepts which provide the basis for those promises. But why start now? Why should those promises be more important now than they were a few years ago?

We will do what we said we would do. Wrong! We're not doing what we said we would do back when we organized the Social Security Administration. Instead, our politicians have been cannibalizing the social security financial coffers to fund other projects, practically since Day One. Old folks are biting the bullet because we aren't doing what we said we would do.

We will protect the interests of the people of the United States. Wrong! Whose interests were we protecting when we allowed thousands of United States citizens to be killed during the Viet-Nam Conflict? Whose interests have we been protecting in Iraq, Iran, Pakistan, Afghanistan, or a dozen other FOREIGN countries where military victims have been sacrificed to serve the secret agendas of the idiot bureaucrats in Washington?

Whose interests have we been protecting by sending billions of dollars in aid to foreign countries (some of whom have nothing but hatred for us, incidentally) while we allow homeless Americans to starve and die of exposure on the streets of our cities?

We will look out for the welfare of our fellow human beings. Wrong! WHICH of our fellow human beings were we looking out for when we bailed out a bunch of large banks, real estate firms, corporations and the automobile industry? Do I not qualify as a fellow human being? Nobody bailed out good old Roy. Or any of my family members. Or any of my neighbors out here in the community of Economy. Or anybody that I know of in the town of Atkins. All we got was a heavy tax debt. A tax debt that none of us will ever live long enough to see the resolution of. Even our grandchildren won't see the end of it. It appears that some of those CEO's and corporation presidents qualify as MORE of a fellow human being than we do. Right, we're all equal in the eyes of our benevolent and loving government but, apparently, some are more equal than some others.

If I win the lottery, I may eventually get around to helping people in other countries. After all, I've been to several foreign countries and I enjoyed seeing the sights, learning about their cultures and getting to know the people. With my lottery winnings, I will provide aid and assistance to an ever-widening circle of family, loved ones, friends and neighbors but, first and foremost, I will help those near the center of that circle before I help those at the outer fringes of that circle. That personal policy should be our national policy.

Sure, let's look out for the welfare of our fellow human beings. Let's help everybody that deserves help. But let's START right here, first. Let's solve the problems in our own house before we start trying to solve the problems in somebody else's house.

Chapter 48

Owe Me a Living

During a news broadcast on 19 Sept 2012, it was reported that one of the presidential candidates said that 47% of our population thinks the government owes them a living. I have always believed that we had too many politicians but I didn't realize they comprised that large a percentage of our populace. I'm not sure if they actually specified the identity of the 47% group but I'm sure he must have been referring to politicians because they are the only people I know who think the government owes them a living.

I have recently started receiving social security payments but that isn't free money. I paid in to the social security fund during my entire working life. And I am still paying in because I have a part-time job so contributions to social security are automatically taken out of my paycheck. What I'm receiving from social security is a return on my life-long investment, so that doesn't qualify as free money.

When I qualify for Medicare, there will be a hundred dollars per month deducted from my social security check to pay for it, so that doesn't qualify as free money, either. Plus, Medicare pays for only about 80% of my part B medical expenses and for nothing else, so I'm not getting very much value for my money.

I don't get food stamps and the government doesn't help me pay my rent, my utilities, the repairs on my old truck or the gasoline to keep it running, so if any of that counts as free money, none of it comes my way. But enough about me. I'm just an average citizen.

Now, let's consider the average Washington politician. You need to understand that these people need only serve one term (four years) and they will receive their wages for the rest of their lives, whether or not they actually accomplished anything during those four years. They made that decision and voted on it for themselves. Of course, these figures are from November 2011. The numbers have probably gone up, since then. I can absolutely guarantee they didn't go down.

President	$450,000 per year for life
Speaker of the House	$223,500 per year for life
Majority/Minority Leader	$193,400 per year for life
Member of House/Senate	$174,000 per year for life
Social Security Senior Citizen	$ 12,000 per year for life (average)

What I would like to know, but could not find out, is this: If a member of the House of Representatives becomes a Senator (or vice versa) and serves four years in each job, does he receive the paycheck for BOTH jobs for life? Or if a member of Congress becomes President, does he still receive lifetime paychecks as a Congressman AND a lifetime paycheck as a President? After all, by their reckoning, if they served 4 years in each category, they qualified for both paychecks. In any other field of endeavor, it would be called double-dipping, but since they make their own rules and they are the ones who vote for their own rules, the answer may very well be YES.

The senior citizen has to work until he is AT LEAST 62 years of age before he starts drawing his money. Politicians probably do a victory dance and give each other "high fives" every time a citizen dies at the age of 61 because he paid taxes and social security payments throughout his entire life and now they don't have to give back any of it.

But wait, there's more. Politicians get free medical, free dental, free postal services, free parking, free shoe shines. They don't make payments on their "official" vehicle or for repairs to the vehicle. They don't pay for the gas that goes into the tank. They don't even have to stand at the gas pump, shaking their heads in dismay while they fill the tank. Their chauffeur takes care of that.

Politicians take every opportunity to arrange boondoggles for their own state or region to ensure future votes and award contracts to people who make substantial contributions to their campaign fund while taking free trips, gifts, contributions and favors from special interest groups and PAC's. They take their families and staff with them on "fact-finding missions" to exotic locales. Missions which have nothing to do with the actual finding of facts but which are paid for with taxpayers' money. They vote pay raises for themselves while they exempt themselves from paying taxes on the "second homes" they supposedly have to maintain while they are in the DC area, away from their home states, allegedly serving the American People. They exempt themselves and their staffs from the wage and hiring laws which they dictate to private businesses. They are all Hill Hypocrites.

Politicians forget very quickly how difficult it is to make ends meet. For example, the President doesn't pay rent or utility bills, not even for that part of the White House that is designated as his private family quarters. If the water heater or the air conditioner fails, he doesn't have to pay for repairs or replacement parts. He doesn't have to pull out his wallet to put the groceries on the table. His family doesn't have to do the cooking and cleaning of their private family quarters--and he doesn't have to pay the wages of the cooks, servants, maids or helpers who do take care of those things. He doesn't have to pay home insurance (or renter's insurance since no President actually owns the White House). He doesn't have to make car payments or pay car insurance or even buy fuel for the vehicles he rides in (but then again, no other politician has to do those things, either).

Whenever the President has a "date night" with his wife, he may spend anywhere from $26,000 to $60,000 dollars of taxpayers' money. And I'm not talking about JUST Mister Obama. All Presidents flourish under these same conditions.

But I have picked on him, enough, already. Other members of the federal aristocracy are equally callous about how we are affected when they squander our tax dollars. For example, federal judges use our money to build castles and monuments to themselves, with courtrooms that have mahogany paneling and marble floors and have their private chambers luxuriously furnished with high quality furniture and complete kitchens (places where a family of four would be proud to live).

During the past few years, our politicians have given over fifteen billion dollars to Russia while Russia's leaders have siphoned off major portions of this money and put it into numbered personal bank accounts in various parts of the world.

Our politicians have spent many billions of dollars rebuilding Iraq--and we didn't even have any business being there, in the first place. The United States pays ONE THIRD of the cost of the United Nations peacekeeping operations--and those operations aren't even effective. Our country has forgiven billions upon billions of dollars in war debts from other countries which never even tried to pay the interest on those debts, in the first place. We have spent uncountable billons rebuilding other countries which lost previous wars to us--countries which were (and still are) our bitter enemies.

These things I've mentioned aren't even a molecule on the tip of the iceberg of the many ways in which politicians have literally stabbed America in the back. And yet, they belly up to the national money trough and root around for every dollar, every benefit, every perk with which they can line their own pockets. Politicians are the ones who think the government owes them a living.

They allow their greed to influence them to take actions which ensure their personal wealth and well-being, so I consider them to be lacking in honor and integrity. They allow their secret agendas to influence them to give away billions of dollars to foreign countries (even to countries that are openly our avowed enemies) instead of directing that money toward improving the lives of American citizens. Therefore, I consider them to be lacking in a sense of common decency (not to mention outright disloyalty to the USA).

On 13 July 2011, I heard the President say, on television, that he could not guarantee that the social security checks for August would be sent out unless Congress agreed to raise the national debt limit. He said the money would simply not be in the coffers. At the time, it was my opinion that somebody should explain to the President that the social security money should not be affected by the national debt. I had been paying in money to the social security system all of my working life, as had millions upon millions of other REAL Americans. The only reason the money isn't there is because the politicians have been siphoning it off and dipping into it at every possible opportunity to fund other "pet" programs. If a board member of a private company did something like that with the retirement fund money from his company's funds, he would have gone to jail forever for embezzlement. Apparently, stealing is legal only when politicians do it.

Instead of threatening to withhold social security checks, I would have liked to hear the President say this, "I can't guarantee that pay checks will be sent to ANY politician, including myself, until Congress comes up with a sensible, responsible, viable solution to the financial crisis which we politicians have all created". I bet that would have fostered a solution, practically overnight.

The median wage in the United States is $50,000. The median wage in Arkansas is $41,000. There is only one state in the union that has a lower median wage. Obviously, most of us here are already in dire straits and, unlike the politicians, we still have to pay the usual bills, such as rent, utilities and insurance while trying to put enough food on the table to live. So imagine the hopelessness of a social security senior citizen with a fixed income of only $12,000 when the President threatened to withhold even that little bit.

When I became an officer in the United States Marine Corps many decades ago, I took an oath to defend the Constitution against all enemies, foreign and domestic. But really, by their own actions, the politicians have proven themselves to be the most significant threat to our country and our way of life. THEY are the domestic enemies I should have been defending my country against. We common people need to have another "tea party" but not in Boston...I suggest we have it on the Potomac. And instead of throwing tea into the water, maybe we could throw politicians, instead.

I may get charged with treason and be investigated by the FBI as a militant subversive with mental defects and they might spend another million dollars to send a bunch of idiot government agents down here to see what kind of rebellion I might be fomenting. But I actually love my country. It's just my country's politicians I can't stand. And I don't care if they are Democrat, Republican, or Independent. They're all politicians. Therefore, in my humble opinion, they are all equally despicable.

Chapter 49

Fair Play

In Dec 2012, a television news item noted that some slogans being displayed in public aren't fair in regard to their content and Congress might get involved to ensure equality on both sides of the issue. The particular subject cited was the plethora of decals that deal with the anti/pro abortion issue. In a similar vein, the commentator joked that if someone is going to display a decal that advocates saving sea turtles, there should be an equal number of decals displayed that advocate killing sea turtles. In the interest of fair play.

I'm all in favor of fair play, but do we need a law that dictates a policy of fair play? If I display a decal that says, "Just say No to drugs", will I then be required to also display a decal that says, "Just say Yes to drugs", in accordance with whatever would be required by the new law enacted by our idiot politicians? In the interest of fair play.

And if fair play is going to be mandated by law in one regard, what about all the other circumstances where fair play would then become necessary? For instance, we have all those ads that advocate smoking cures (patches, etc). I've never smoked but it seems as if we would be required to bring back cigarette commercials. In the interest of fair play.

NASCAR has some very explicit rules regarding what can and cannot be done to race cars, so that nobody has an unfair advantage and at the horse races, some horses are required to carry extra weight if the jockey doesn't weigh a specified amount. Therefore, in the

Olympics, some runners should be required to carry extra weight if they are skinnier than some of the other runners. Also, since some of the runners are taller than some others, their longer legs might give them an unfair advantage over shorter runners, so their finish line should be moved farther down the track. In the interest of fair play.

Some work places give maternity leave to expectant mothers, who are allowed to take time off from work to deliver (and nurture) their babies, knowing that their job will be waiting for them when they return. But women who never have any children should also be allowed to take off from work an equal amount of time, with the same job security assurances. In the interest of fair play.

As a veteran of the Viet-Nam war, I am allowed to display a special license plate on my truck, as are veterans of other military conflicts. However, I actually own two trucks, but I am allowed only one specialty license plate. I told the lady at the revenue office that I should be allowed two veteran's plates because I went to Viet-Nam twice. She said that didn't count because it was only one theater of operations. The fact that I skipped over into Cambodia and Laos a couple of times didn't sway her opinion but I still insist that I should be allowed two veteran plates. In the interest of fair play.

And what about all those cowards who evaded military service during the 60's (my era) by going to Canada? They should be allowed to purchase specialty license plates, too. But instead of saying "Viet-Nam War Veteran", their tags could say "Draft-dodger".In the interest of fair play.

If I get a ticket for speeding, shouldn't the policeman be required to issue a speeding ticket to himself, too? After all, he had to go faster than I was going in order to catch up with me. In fact, if he had to cut across a median and weave through traffic, then he was probably also guilty of reckless driving. In the interest of fair play.

And the companies that make those political bumper stickers. If they produce a bunch of stickers for one political party, wouldn't they be required to make an equal number of stickers for the other political party, not to mention all those independent candidates? In the interest of fair play.

Finally, our politicians. (They probably hoped I was going to refrain from mentioning them, this time). I'm not smart enough to know all of the implications of the end-of-year tax problems and I'm not smart enough to know who's right or wrong. But I am smart enough to know that NOBODY is either 100% right OR wrong all the time, so if those idiots in Washington can't figure out how to keep our economy from going over a fiscal cliff, then we should legally be allowed to push all of them over a physical cliff. In the interest of fair play.

Chapter 50

Separation of Church and State

Our current government supposedly operates under the premise that church and state should be kept separate. In fact, our leaders presumably go to great lengths to ensure that this is so. What I don't understand is the process by which they are trying to make this so. For example, children aren't allowed to pray in school but every session of Congress starts with a benediction. Maybe I'm just not smart enough to follow their reasoning but, even though most schools are mandated by the government, school children would certainly not be considered as much a part of "the State" as congressmen would be.

When a President is inaugurated, he puts his hand on a Bible to take his oath of office. In fact, the last time Mister Obama was sworn in, he put his hand on TWO Bibles. In order to ensure the separation of Church and State, maybe the incoming President should just put his hand on a copy of the Constitution, or perhaps the Bill of Rights.

When I became an officer in the United States Marine Corps, my oath of office ended with the phrase, "So help me, God". I became a leader in a military organization, an organization in which I would kill the enemy--and I would direct my troops to kill the enemy--in order to protect and defend the Constitution (to wit, the State) but I was invoking the aid of God (to wit, the Church) to assist me in carrying out my lethal duties.

So, considering the fact that elected officials in the United States (Presidents, members of Congress, Governors, well, all of them), federal appointees (Supreme Court Justices, Judges, Cabinet members, etc.), and members of the armed forces (undeniably, a part of the government) all take an oath, while either placing their hand on a Bible or otherwise invoking the aid of God to guide and aid them in their various chosen fields of endeavor, why do we insist that there should be a separation of Church and State when it is so very obvious that there is not?

"In God we trust" That's what is printed on all of our money, which is designed and printed, or minted, by the government. A government whose Founding Fathers used their religious faith as the cornerstone of the principles which established and ordained the new government. That same government which extols and celebrates the fact that we were created and designed in such a way that we would willingly govern ourselves in a manner that would be pleasing to our Creator.

So, what's the big deal about this so-called separation of Church and State, anyway? The American Civil Liberties Union got excited over the fact that a prayer was spoken over a loudspeaker before a summertime rodeo in Jackson, Wyoming, as reported in the Russellville *Courier* newspaper on 11 Jan 2013? The ACLU claimed this was a violation of the separation of Church and State.

The article didn't specify whether or not an elected official was the speaker when the public prayer was given but it did note that the town council took steps to make sure the prayer was nonsectarian, which means it was 'not restricted to members of one religious denomination, but open to all'. Maybe that will shut up the ACLU. Their name should probably be changed to the Anti-American Civil Liberties Union. For many years, they have often been in the news and, in every instance, their stance has definitely been based on anti-American tenets and suppositions. In my humble opinion, it seems as though their purpose has always been not to defend the Constitution, but to destroy it.

On 16 Jan 2013, in an article written by Mark Darr, the Arkansas Lieutenant Governor, he pointed out that there is a Bible on his desk in the Senate--it has been there since 1943--and that it is a good reminder to all of the Senators of our nation's religious heritage and of the moral compass that exists within its pages. He also stated that he has an open Bible on a coffee table in his office and says that both of these Bibles provide guidance in the daily performance of his governmental duties.

But it appears that "the Church" itself can sometimes be its own worst enemy, as indicated by an article in the Arkansas *Democrat*

Gazette newspaper on 8 Feb 2013. Why else would the Reverend Bob Morris of Christ the King Lutheran Church in Newtown, Connecticut be reprimanded by the Lutheran Church-Missouri Synod for participating in an interfaith vigil after the Sandy Hook massacre? Church officials decided that he inadvertently gave the impression he condoned joint worship by offering the benediction at the event with other religious leaders for the elementary school shooting victims.

Those church officials must be complete idiots. It was an INTERFAITH vigil. It was JOINT worship. I'm no genius, by any stretch of the imagination, but I would think the terms 'interfaith' and 'joint worship' would mean that a member of ANY religious order would be welcome at the vigil, whether he be Protestant, Catholic, Jewish, Buddhist or whatever. The members of each religious group should have been happy, nay delighted, that they could all stand together for a common cause.

But I am truly mystified by Islam, the religion of Muslims. An article in the Arkansas *Democrat Gazette* dated 8 Feb 2013 stated that Egyptian clerics urged killing and rape. This is a religion that teaches adherents that it is okay to blow themselves up as long as they take as many non-Islamists as possible with them when they die. This supposedly guarantees them a spot in Paradise. What kind of stupidity is that? Call me naïve and misguided, if you wish, but it is my understanding that a religion should teach people to REFRAIN from killing and raping rather than justifying-even glorifying-such practices. But it's okay with me if the Muslims want to believe that Mohammed wrote the Koran in Allah's EXACT words as told to him by the Angel Gabriel during the 7th century. After all, Christians believe that the Bible was written over an extended period of many, many years by men who were inspired directly by God. Fair's fair. The major difference, as I understand it, is that Christianity teaches peace, love and brotherhood while Islam insists that all non-believers must be converted, subjugated or destroyed.

But back to the business of separation of Church and State. An article in the Arkansas *Democrat Gazette* dated 8 Feb 2013 discussed the 61st National Prayer Breakfast in Washington, our nation's capital, where political leaders, including our own President Obama, gathered to pray. There were more than 1,000 guests from every state and from 160 countries, including the Prime Ministers of Serbia and the

Democratic Republic of the Congo. It was sponsored by House and Senate prayer groups and by The Fellowship Foundation, a politically connected Virginia nonprofit group. The article further pointed out that each Wednesday morning, senators meet in the Capitol to pray.

So, for the last 61 years, a bunch of politicians (the State) have gathered together to invoke the power of prayer (the Church) in the very seat of our political leadership. Does this sound like separation of Church and State? Where was the ACLU? Why weren't they right in the midst of this assemblage, screaming about the violation of separation policy? Maybe they prefer to pick their fights with lesser mortals, like the town council in Jackson, Wyoming, where they think they might be more easily able to run roughshod over their victims. I'd be willing to bet, with absolute certainty of winning my bet, that if a bunch of school kids tried to have a prayer breakfast, the ACLU would be all over them.

Personally, I'm highly in favor of a national prayer breakfast but it should not be once a year. Our leaders should pray every day. Maybe there would be fewer of them willing to trade political favors for votes or even for financial remuneration, fewer of them who avoid any public controversy which might deplete their voter base, fewer of them to stick their noses into foreign affairs and conflicts which have nothing to do with us, fewer of them to give favorable treatment to extremist groups like tobacco lobbyists, homosexual groups and gun lobbyists. Yes, our leaders should definitely pray more. They don't do very well, on their own. God knows, they need all the help they can get.

But wait, they DO pray every day. Every session of Congress is opened with a prayer. The ACLU should be storming the doors every single morning, protesting the actions of our political leaders (the State) who are praying for divine guidance from the Supreme Being (the Church), in violation of the separation of Church and State.

P. S. When I was in the Marine Corps, I attended many prayer breakfasts, at various commands and duty stations, sometimes once each month. I would gather in the unit mess hall (now called a dining facility) with my fellow officers, meeting in advance of the official start of our various daily duties, to celebrate the existence of the Supreme Being, a Deity who espouses the finer traits of peace and love. Most of us were combat veterans, and most of us were in uniform, wearing our service ribbons, medals and decorations with rifle and pistol qualification badges to indicate that we were warriors who had gone in harm's way in order that so many others (loved ones, families, friends, civilians) might be able to enjoy the benefits (like peace and love) that our sacrifices had made possible. Gathered there for a simple prayer breakfast, hoping that God would bless our efforts in the service of those precious others. I can just imagine the bedlam that would surely have ensued if any given number of ACLU members might have attempted to break in on our meeting in a hopeless attempt to protest our violation of the concept of separation of Church and State. I would pity the fools.

Chapter 51

Humanitarian Aid

On 20 Feb 2013, a tv news item indicated that we had given 385 million dollars in humanitarian aid to Syria. This news item was not the subject of conversation by any of the news commentators. It was nothing more than a small blurb of information that was scrolled across the bottom of the screen, almost as if they are required by some edict that forces them to present this particular news item to the public but they are not required to actually comment on it. And it wasn't scrolled across there by itself, preceded by flashing asterisks to attract our attention to it. It was added in with some other information.

I may have my priorities out of order but I consider 385 million dollars to be important enough to warrant at least a casual mention by one of the news commentators. Especially when all of that is American tax dollars going to people who are not Americans. I don't mean to sound cold and callous but that's an awful lot of humanitarianism. I don't know anything about foreign policy but we are apparently the only nation on earth that routinely practices that type of philanthropy. Question: Were there any Syrian dollars that came our way to assist in the recovery of the areas that were devastated during the storms along our upper east coast? More to the point, have there been any Syrian dollars sent our way after ANY of our natural disasters during the past hundred years? Or after any of our manmade disasters, for that matter? I didn't see any memorial wreaths from Syria after the school shooting in Newtown. None that were publicized, anyway.

Before anybody decides that I have some sort of personal grudge against Syria, let me mention that I also did not hear of any donations from any other countries, either. Not even from countries to which we have given billions upon billions of dollars in foreign aid, humanitarian or otherwise, in the very recent past. Somebody tell me if I am wrong. If I missed an article in the newspaper that pointed out some country that tried to help us in any way during the past hundred years, then remind me of it, so I can apologize.

In the United States, there are 16 million children going hungry every day. Right here in the land of milk and honey, where a cornucopia of excess spills over constantly, but it seems to spill over somewhere outside of our national community. Excuse me for sounding like an isolationist but I would like to know if ANY of our idiot politicians might just happen to think that 16 million hungry American kids may be a few too many.

As an individual, I'm not an isolationist. I do favors and good deeds for my neighbors out here in the country quite often but I'm just as likely to help somebody who lives fifty miles away, if I'm in the right place at the right time and have the wherewithal. But if I have only five cans of pork and beans, eight fish sticks and one loaf of bread--and it's still six days until payday--I can't give away very much. Not even to my closest neighbors.

By the same token we, as a nation, can't afford to keep giving. Sure, we can help a few. And we can help a little. But we can't help everybody. We can't take care of the whole world any more than I can take care of all my neighbors. The United States has deep pockets. But they're not bottomless pockets. Our national debt is figured in the TRILLIONS of dollars. If I write one bad check, I could wind up in jail. How many bad checks do our politicians have to write before we take away their pens and slap them on the wrists? This may sound unique and controversial but.....let the buck stop here.

Chapter 52

Who's Accountable

On 6 March 2013, while watching a news program, I learned that the Inspector General had determined that eight billion dollars was wasted or had not been accounted for during the process of rebuilding Iraq. That's eight billion with a B. if that's the amount that's MISSING, how much did we actually commit to that project? In my humble opinion, the missing money, by itself, is an astronomical amount, so the overall amount spent must be a total that even God would consider to be excessive. Besides, nobody ever asked my opinion regarding whether or not we should be paying for the rebuilding of Iraq, just as I was never consulted regarding whether or not we should have been involved with what was going on over there, in the first place.

And this missing money was not even considered important enough to be the subject of conversation by any of the commentators. Just like the money I discussed in the previous chapter, this money was merely the subject of an informational blurb that was scrolled across the bottom of the screen while the commentators discussed other stuff. Like before, maybe they were obliged, by some regulation, to present the info about the missing money but they wanted to do so in such a way that it might not be noticed by the public because it was included among some other information in those scrolled items.

If the money was channeled through a numbered Swiss bank account, I might be able to understand how we could have some difficulty in tracking it down. But if the money was United States government funds, wouldn't it be logical to assume that it would have been transferred from one responsible government agency to some other responsible government agency? Surely, we didn't just put the cash into a metal shipping container the size of a semi-trailer and load it onto a ship! Okay, actually, it would have be a lot of shipping containers.

Is our government really that irresponsible with the taxpayers' money? Oh sorry, that is a dumb question. Yes, they are! But there has to be some sort of trail we can follow. There has to be somebody to whom we can go and say something like, "Okay, you were the last one with it. What happened to it?" There must be somebody who's accountable.

Actually, I know who's responsible. The President. He's the top dog. He has the final word. He's the one who should have to pay the price for the mistakes made by his subordinates. If he wants to point fingers at a select group and insist that they also be punished because they were the ones who actually mishandled the funds, that's all well and good but, whatever they did, they did with his blessings, so they can be considered as co-conspirators, but he is still ultimately responsible. He owes me eight billion dollars.

I mean me, the taxpayer, generically speaking. My personal share would be quite small. The President would probably insist that he is not to blame for the crimes committed by the people under his command but I contend that, if Lieutenant Calley can be charged, prosecuted and convicted as being solely responsible for the alleged atrocities committed by members of his platoon in My Lai in Viet-Nam in 1968 simply because he was the man in charge, then the President should be held accountable for the criminal activities of the people in his administration. After all, he is the Ultimate Platoon Commander. He is the man who's accountable.

Chapter 53

Pass the Buck

Earlier this year (2013), while watching a news broadcast, I learned that a guy sued and won over 7 million dollars because he developed popcorn lung after eating three bags of microwave popcorn every day for ten years.

But wait, here are a few more examples of "stupidity equals profit". A heavy smoker died from lung cancer and his widow sued the tobacco company. A man got drunk in a bar and died in a car wreck. His family sued the bar owner for selling liquor to the man. A lady sued a fast food chain because she burned herself after removing the lid from a container of coffee and placing the container between her knees while driving. A man sued the owner of a house he had just burgled because he got stuck in the garage while making his escape. A woman sued the manufacturer of a mobile home because it ran off the freeway after she set the cruise control and left the driver's seat to make a sandwich.

These are real cases. I can provide names and dates in all of these cases, if necessary, and I could fill a lot more pages with examples of people who do equally stupid things but still manage to find a way to make somebody else responsible for the consequences.

How can any judge allow these frivolous cases to go forward in the court systems? And how can the juries approve the outlandish awards that are given? They're all so incredibly stupid, if I didn't know any better, I would think the judges and jury members are all former politicians.

If a smoker can sue a tobacco company, why can't he also sue the store that sold the cigarettes, or the trucker who delivered the cigarettes to the store, or the farmer who grew the tobacco leaves? If a drunk can sue a bar for selling liquor, he might as well also sue the distillery that made the liquor and the farmer who grew the corn.

But why should a bartender be responsible for gauging the sobriety of his customers? If a bartender sold me even one beer, he would be guilty of creating a public safety hazard because I never drank in my life, so one beer would make me an unsafe driver. How is any bartender supposed to know stuff like that?

So could a parent sue the owner of a candy store for the cost of a child's dental work? After all, if he keeps selling candy to him simply because the kid has money available to pay for it, he is responsible for the cavities. He should put a limit on his customers, for their own good. Forget that he's in business to make a profit and selling equals profit.

If I go to Las Vegas and lose all my money at the gambling tables, can I sue the owner of the casino because he didn't tell his dealers to make a judgment call on when I have spent enough? They should cut me off before I exceed my financial limit. It doesn't matter that they have no way of knowing what my limit is. How dare they continue to take my money simply because I'm stupid enough to keep offering it?

We have car doors that won't open if we are too drunk to punch in the right code. We have car ignitions that won't start if we don't pass a breathalyzer test. We have air bags that protect us if we're too drunk, too stupid, too careless or simply too unlucky to avoid an accident. We have a multitude of products that have an incredible number of gadgets, safeguards and devices whose sole function is to protect us from our own idiocy. But somehow, some of us manage to either embarrass, injure, maim and even kill ourselves, in spite of all this. But no matter what, we can still pass the buck. Surely somebody else (anybody else) must be at fault.

In case you may be wondering what this has to do with my upbringing, my point here is simple: Mom and Dad raised us kids in such a way that we are willing to stand up and take responsibility for our mistakes and it really torques my jaws to think about the way manufacturers of all kinds of products have to take all kinds of precautionary measures and install numerous safety features to protect the public from its own stupidity--this drives the prices of these products up far beyond my ability to absorb the financial strain. So don't get upset when I say I have no patience with idiots. The lady who burns herself with hot coffee is stupid but the politicians who pass laws that provide that lady with an opportunity to pass the buck are even more stupid than she is, not to mention the judge (another politician) who allows her lawsuit to proceed, tying up the court's time and assets and wasting taxpayer money to process the paperwork. The way I figure it, no matter how many idiots are out here in public, it's the politicians who are actually at the root of the problem, which proves my point that none of them are worth one percent of what they cost us.

But wait, there is one instance where passing the buck may be a legitimate course of action. I want to cash in on some of this easy money so maybe I could sue the education system for mental stress, anguish and anxiety because I am left-handed. You see, for the first five years of my schooling, I was forced to sit in a single pedestal desk which was designed for right-handed students. Back in those days, the school desks were all built the same way. Since lefties make up less than ten percent of the population, this practice constitutes discrimination against a minority. Therefore, I can blame all of my aberrant behavior as an adult on the trauma of having to start out left-handed in a right-handed world. Uh-oh, no, wait a minute, my master plan may not work because this might mean I would have to sue God for making me left-handed, in the first place. He might not let me pass the buck.

Chapter 54

According to the Bible

Psalms 62:12--And loving kindness is Thine, O Lord, for Thou dost recompense a man according to his work.

Proverbs 24:12--Does He not consider it Who weighs the hearts? And does He not know it Who keeps your soul? And will He not render to man according to his work?

Isaiah 59:18--According to their deeds, so He will repay.

Romans 2:6--Who will render to every man according to his deeds.

Revelation 20:12--And I saw the dead, the great and the small, standing before the throne, and books were opened; and another book was opened, which is the book of life, and the dead were judged from the things which were written in the books, according to their deeds.

Revelation 20:13--And the sea gave up the dead which were in it, and death and Hades gave up the dead which were in them, and they were judged, every one of them, accord-ing to their deeds.

Matthew 5:3--Blessed are the poor in spirit, for theirs is the Kingdom of Heaven.

Matthew 5:4--Blessed are they that mourn, for they shall be comforted.

Matthew 5:5--Blessed are the gentle, for they shall inherit the earth.

Matthew 5:6--Blessed are they which do hunger and thirst after
          righteousness, for they shall be filled.
Matthew 5:7--Blessed are the merciful, for they shall receive mercy.

Matthew 5:8--Blessed are the pure in heart, for they shall see God.

Matthew 5:9--Blessed are the peacemakers, for they shall be called sons
          of God.

Matthew 5:10-Blessed are they which are persecuted for righteousness'
          sake, for theirs is the kingdom of Heaven.

Matthew 5:11-You are the salt of the earth.

What does all this mean, all this talk about "according to their deeds"? The deeds which might count against us are supposedly wiped out if we accept Jesus---aren't they?

To further cloud the issue, why would all these blessings be bestowed on people in so many different categories if they are going to be condemned to Hell, anyway, just because they may not have gone through the process of accepting Jesus?

Well, those who are "poor in spirit" and those who are "persecuted for righteousness' sake" may be alright because "theirs is the kingdom of Heaven". I don't know if it would be a safe assumption but I would assume that those two groups will go to Heaven. If I'm to believe what I read in the Bible, that's the way those two statements read.

However, the other "blessed" categories don't fill me with a great deal of confidence. For example, those who mourn are blessed "for they shall be comforted". that's all well and good but it doesn't say that they will be comforted eternally or that their comforting will take place in Heaven.

Then there's the meek, who "shall inherit the earth". They may be blessed but that doesn't necessarily mean they're going to Heaven. And the earth is going to be destroyed, anyway. I don't know exactly where the Bible says that the earth isn't going to last forever but I know it says "this earth, too, shall pass away", so it wouldn't really be all that great to inherit the earth.

What about those "which do hunger and thirst after righteousness"? What good would it do them to be filled, if they aren't standing inside Heaven, at the time?

The merciful may have a chance to go to Heaven but "obtaining mercy" doesn't mean they are guaranteed to obtain that much mercy.

The "pure in heart" may very well get to "see God" but it won't do them any good to see God if they are standing in the pits of Hell when His vision appears to them.

It won't do the "peacemakers" any good to be "called Children of God", if they are going to be condemned to damnation simply because they haven't kneeled at an altar.

Blessed are all these categories, no doubt about that, because Jesus said so. But all of the blessings that could possibly be bestowed on us are worth absolutely nothing if they aren't going to open the Pearly Gates for us. And He didn't say they would, specifically.

So, what's the bottom line, here? If I'm going to be judged according to my deeds, was it a waste of time and effort to accept Jesus? And if Jesus' blood wipes away my evil deeds, why does the Bible repeatedly insist that I'm going to be judged "according to my deeds"? And don't try to tell me that pertains only to the people under Mosaic Law who were around before Jesus came along to die for our sins because there are references in the New Testament about being judged "according to our deeds". Which is it?

I'm told that the Bible doesn't contradict itself. If it doesn't, then why is it telling me that I can only be saved by having my evil deeds cancelled out (at least, up to that point) by having my soul washed in the blood of Jesus Christ through confession and baptism and yet, it also tells me that I will be "judged according to my deeds".

I'm sorry. I don't mean to be argumentative and I don't mean to cause friction among the religious orders. I would be only too glad to believe what I read in the Bible but I do respectfully insist on being able to believe ALL that I read in the Bible, which is simply not possible, at least not for me--and I'm the one who's going to be judged, so I have a lot at stake here. Some would say I just need more Bible study and some would say I just need more faith. I simply say I'm like 'Doubting Thomas'. I guess I just need to be able to touch the wound.

Thicker Than Water

Roy Morris

Poems by Roy

Chapter 55

A Transfusion

The world's first blood bank
Was established long ago
Jesus made the first donation
Because he loves us so
His blood is still as fresh today
As it was when He first bled
Though mixed with Jesus' sweat and tears
It's still vital, rich and red
The giving of it cost His life
He knew it would be so
But His Father had commanded
To the Cross He had to go
To accept the offering Jesus made
Is such a simple thing
To the altar on bended knees
Three things you must bring
A penitent heart is one of these
A heart that knows it's worth
A heart that doesn't want to fear
When it's time to leave this earth
A second thing is a body of flesh
That knows it's frail and weak
A body that is now willing to bow
The Master's Grace to seek

The third requirement is a mind
That accepts, by faith and trust
That resurrection is now assured
Even after it's turned to dust
A penitent heart
A bended knee
A mind that seeks eternity
By His blood
These things will ensure
That the soul is washed
Clean and pure
If you need a transfusion
Then get it now
Repent, be faithful
And ready to bow
This blood bank
Will never run dry
It's available for free
Until the minute you die
So bow and be saved
You'll never be billed
Jesus prepaid the price
Up there on that hill

Chapter 56

All

All that I am
Or shall ever hope to be
All that I have
Or shall ever receive
I will give to thee
If you will give to me
The joy and the ecstasy
Of living and loving faithfully
Until I find eternity

Published
Atkins Chronicle
27 Sep 95

Published
National Library of Poetry
(Tomorrow Never Knows)
Fall 95

Chapter 57

An Uncle, Once More

For many years I was alone
My nieces and nephews
All grown up and gone
The girls were beautiful
Smart and sweet
The boy was handsome
The world at his feet
But no longer "kids"
Too big now to play
Toy trains and dolls
Were all put away
No more rides on the "horsey"
Across the living room rug
No more bedtime stories
No sweet goodnight hugs
Then you came along
And made it all new
It got started again
Because now there was you
A new make-believe world
With a princess…and dragons
And I pulled you around
In a little red wagon

We watched kiddy movies
And a bunch of cartoons
And we played on the floor
With a bunch of balloons
So I'm needed again
Now it's just like before
There's a child to take care of
I'm an uncle, once more

The New Batch (from the 90's)	The Original Batch (from the 60's and 80's)
Diana	Jo
Jessica	Laura
Rachel	Jason
Matthew	Gini
	Renea

Chapter 58

Barbed Wire Boogie

When you work with barbed wire
You'd better have a care
The points are sharp
They're worse than darts
You'll leave some skin on there
A fence line is a favorite place
For briars and brambles to grow
They'll whip and snap
And lash about
And cause your blood to flow
If you get past the busy mass
And haven't felt their points
Then poison ivy will fill the gap
You'll itch from joint to joint
So if your boss sends you across
To the other side of the fence
Don't take a chance
Climbing through that dense
Tangle of brush and wire
Don't tempt your fate
Go find a gate
You'll be better off, by far

Chapter 59

Dying

Dying can't really be so hard
When you get down to it
It's just a simple letting go
Everyone goes through it
No need to worry
No need to fret
You'll find a way
On that, I'll bet
So just relax
And close your eyes
I know you can endure it
'cause after all
It ain't so hard
Even babies do it

For my brother	Cecil Ray	08-16-42 to ??-??-46
For my daughter	Brandie Lynn	05-28-80 to 08-29-80
For my niece	Autumn Diane	05-22-95 to 05-22-95
For my niece	Jessica Marie	01-12-98 to 12-03-98
For my great-niece	Ashley Rose	03-15-01 to 04-16-01
For my niece	Lisa Ann	11-06-71 to 08-01-03

Published
Famous Poets Society
(New Millennium Poets)
Fall 02

Chapter 60

Rain

Rain, rain don't stay away
Can't hardly wait another day
Need rain to make my pasture green
Need rain to make my windshield clean
Don't rush on in and then just blow
We need rain regular soft and slow
Sunshine is fine in it's own way
But not forever and a day
Don't mean to gripe don't mean to fuss
Just need a little pity on us
I'll rain-dance like a Cherokee
'cause there's a bit of Indian in me
Whatever it takes I'll give it a try
To make some rain fall from the sky

29 July 2012

Published
Atkins Chronicle
1 Aug 2012

Chapter 61

See who catches hell

I'm not allowed to drive the train
The whistle I can't blow
I'm not allowed to decide
How fast the train will go
I don't say how many cars
From engine to caboose
And if the load's too heavy
Which ones will be cut loose
I'm not allowed to debate
Just where the train will stop
Or when consolidating routes
Which ones we'll have to drop
I don't get to holler "board"
Or do conductor-type things
I don't get to punch the tickets
The lantern I can't swing
I'm not allowed to hold the oil can
Or ring the little bell
But let the damn thing
Jump the tracks
And see who catches hell

January 1982

This was inspired by a four-line poem that I saw in the office of the Company Executive Officer of Headquarters and Service Company, Supply Battalion at the Marine Corps Base, Camp Lejeune, North Carolina, where I served as a Platoon Commander. In the military chain of command, a Company Executive Officer is second-in-command to a Company Commander. In this particular case, both the CO and the XO were really good people and both had a good sense of humor. I don't know who wrote the original few lines of the poem or how many versions may be in existence out there somewhere. But from those four lines I saw, the above poem is my version.

Original anonymous version

I'm not allowed to drive the train
Or ring the little bell
But let the damn thing jump the tracks
And see who catches hell

Chapter 62

Seymour

Had a mouse in the bathroom
(he died before he got old)
His favorite hiding place
Was behind the bowl
He thought he was cool
He didn't have a care
He scared all his visitors
While their torsos were bare
He scampered, he scurried
He had lots of guts
Because of his angle
I named him Seymour Butts

Published
National Library of Poetry
(Best Poems of 1996)
Winter 96

Published
Famous Poets Press
(Famous Poets of the Heartland)
Spring 13

Chapter 63

Teenager

These flowers will fade
And wilt when they dry
But my love for you
Will never die
Many years from now
You'll remember when
And you'll be thirteen
All over again
Your 'teens' will go fast
'cause they always do
I hope you'll be happy
That your heartaches are few
I hope you're successful
But don't gloat when you win
One day your opponent
May be your best friend
There'll be "Famous Firsts"
That you'll struggle through
First kiss, first love
First heartbreak, too
But know, through it all
That one thing is true
You'll be in my heart
And on my mind, too

For my niece Diana's 13th birthday, with thirteen yellow roses
For my niece Rachel's 13th birthday, with thirteen yellow roses

When my other nieces turned 13, I was either not much more than just a kid myself or I was working out of state, so I wasn't there for them when I should have been. But now, these two are special to me in my old age…and I'm here.

Chapter 64

Thanks

My gift is my writing
With words that might rhyme
These words represent
My thoughts, prayers and time
The kindness you've shown
To someone in need
Has proven you are
Some good folks, indeed
Your hearts are so filled
With the spirit of giving
Each one of you helps
To make life worth living
If I can't make up for
Your time and your trouble
Then I'll pray that in Heaven
Your rewards will be doubled

Dedicated to (in alphabetical order):   The Burnett Family
The Ennis Family
The Johnston Family
The Morris Family

Of all the people I know who might need help in one form or another, I am absolutely the least deserving to receive help. And yet, of all the people I know who might need help, I am the one who most often receives it.

On rare occasions, I try to do a favor for someone or try to lend a helping hand to a family member, a loved one, a friend or a neighbor… or sometimes, to a complete stranger. But every single time, the favor is somehow returned to me tenfold.

I can't give away my money, my efforts or my time. It always comes back to me.
I give an ounce and receive a pound.
I give a minute and receive an hour.
I give a penny and receive a dollar.
I give an inch and receive a mile.

It's more blessed to give than to receive but how would I know? I'm never allowed to just give without receiving

Chapter 65

The Barn

A barn could be a happy place
Regardless of the season
Folks met there at every chance
For many special reasons
On most farms a big old barn
Was the center of social life
A gathering place to slow the pace
For sweethearts, husbands and wives
The old-fashioned barn dance
Gave a chance for romance
For those who seldom met
If not for the call
Of arcade and mall
We'd all be meeting there, yet

Published
International Library of Poetry
Immortal Verses
Fall 08

Chapter 66

The Old Covered Bridge

The old covered bridge
That spans the creek
Was built many years ago
If that old covered bridge could talk
Like creek water, tales would flow
The bridge has seen many changes
That happened through the years
But change isn't always improvement
If it were human, there'd be tears
Those boards have soaked up memories
Don't doubt that 'cause it's true
But sweetest memories are the ones
Made when the bridge was new
The clip-clop of a horse's hooves
The clatter of a wagon
The squeaking of the harness
All form a sing-song pattern
I believe, although it seems absurd
Those sounds can still be sensed
If not by ear, then by the heart
Of that, I am convinced
Where lovers met and feuds were fought
And many a shiny fish was caught

That bridge has truly seen it all
Both joy and turmoil, too
Although it's gone, it'll always be
A special place for me and you

Circa 1965

Published
Eber & Wein Publishing
In My Lifetime
Feb 13

Chapter 67

The Road

There once was an old dirt road
That's now a tree-lined lane
Those sturdy oaks with low-hung limbs
Once brushed the horses' manes
Those trees provided cover and shade
From sun and wind and weather
And led the way past a school house
Where children once would gather
From two hundred years ago and more
The sounds never really fade
They echo 'round the trees and wait
For visitors to the glade
The school is now a briar patch
It's gone without a trace
A grassy meadow covers the yard
Where children often raced
Their lunch pails waited on a shelf
'till noontime recess came
Then the teacher gave them time
To eat and play their games
After class, the children came
And walked along the road
They shared that space with farmers

Who were traveling with their loads
By horse-drawn wagon and mule pack
Farm produce came and went
Along the road, the ruts were deep
The earth, itself, was bent
Where once the hoof and wagon wheel
Took corn and cotton, beans and hay
Signs of the past are with us, still
'cause ruts remain to show the way

Feb 97

Published
National Library of Poetry
(2001-A Poetic Odyssey)
Spring 01

Chapter 68

Thumb

When your thumb hurts
It makes me sad
'cause I don't like it
When you feel bad
You need your thumb
For the things you do
Like writing poems
And stories too
You need your thumb
To hold a book
Or to help your Grandma
When she cooks

Circa 2001

For the young'uns

Chapter 69

We gunned down Santa Claus

Read this page of abbreviation explanations before you read the poem which follows.

Three sixty about	full security on all 360 degrees of the compass
Eighty-ones	eighty-one millimeter mortars
Ontos	self-propelled rocket launcher
Arty F. O.	forward observer for artillery fire
Flares	booby trapped rockets that shoot up into the air and float back down on small parachutes to give illumination
S. I. D.	Security Intrusion Device that detects movement
Tipsy	AN/TPS-83 (Tipsy) a radio/communication instrument
F. P. L.	Final Protective Line of defense
F. M. F. Pac	Fleet Marine Force Pacific (pronounced FMF Pack)
V. C.	Viet Cong (local irregular insurgent Communist forces)

This poem is somewhat irreverent but it reflects the mind-set I had when I was a very young Marine in Viet-Nam. It is not intended to mock Christmas or Santa Claus. It's just a reflection of some of the many absurdities of survival in a hostile environment.

We Gunned Down Santa Claus   (continued)

Strange things were done
'neath the Viet-Nam sun
But the time that locked my jaws
Was the night 'neath the moon
When the third platoon
Gunned down Santa Claus
It started out right
'twas just another night
We had to spend in the dirt
Security was out
Three-sixty about
With a fifty percent alert
With naval guns and eighty-ones
And tanks laid track to track
An Ontos or so
An arty F. O.
And barrages planned
Back to back
Well, I froze where I stood
When out of the wood
Eight horses came charging along
This may sound like "corn"
But those mustangs had horns
I thought, "Mounted Viet Cong?"
He came our way
In what looked like a sleigh
(you never know what they'll use)
Our flares were tripped
The S. I. D. was flipped
And the "Tipsy" blew a fuse
He continued to close
I shouted, "Who goes?"
Like they do in the movie shows
And the answer I got
Believe it or not
Was a hearty, "Ho, Ho, Ho"

the cannons roared
the eighty-ones soared
the naval guns raised hell
a bright red flare
flew through the air
we fired the F. P. L.
then I yelled, "Cease fire"
the smoke cleared the air
I went to see who was there
my memory started to race
my mind plays games
when it comes to names
but I never forget a face
he was dressed in red
and he looked well-fed
older than most VC I'd seen
he looked right weird
in that long white beard
and he hadn't quite died
when I reached his side
but the end was clearly in sight
so I bent real low
and he whispered real slow
"Merry Christmas to all
and to all a good night"
we should have known
that our 'cools' were blown
when that light in the air we'd seen
those awful red flares
must have been theirs
'cause our flares
would have been green
so, by and by, your kids may cry
'cause there's no toys under the tree
but the word has come back
from F. M. F. Pac
Santa had gone VC

Chapter 70

Young at heart

I have joined a Seniors' Bowling League after more than a 14-year hiatus from the sport. Partially because of the lack of practice, partially because of some injuries and partially because of age, my abilities have severely atrophied. I'm just a mere shadow of the talented bowler of my youth. So, since I still have a good sense of humor and since the bowling league is named "Young at Heart", I have penned the following poem.

Young at Heart (all the other parts are very, very old)

Bowling is a wonderful sport
At which I used to compete
My opponents always feared me
And they went down in defeat
The pins used to shake
The pins used to shudder
The pins used to tremble
When my name was uttered
Awards, rings and patches
And trophies galore
They all came my way
When my ball hit the floor
My skills were many

The legends were true
My talent was awesome
Back when it was new
But now that I'm old
That's all in the past
My good luck is gone
It sure faded fast
Now the pins stand there
And they seem to laugh
They duck out of the way
As my ball rolls past
The girls used to sigh
But now they just giggle
My 5 pin won't fall
It won't even wiggle

Thicker Than Water

Roy Morris

Songs by Roy

Chapter 71

A clone of my own

(sung to the tune of *Home on the Range)*

Oh, give me a clone
A clone of my own
With it's Y chromosome
Changed to an X
It'll be another Roy
But it won't be a boy
It'll be a Roy
Of the opposite sex
Clone, clone of my own
While she's around
I'll never be alone
She'll be faithful and true
And I'll never be blue
'cause you know you'll
Like someone who's you

Circa 1966

Chapter 72

Ballad of Roy Morris

Sung to the tune of *The Ballad of Davy Crockett* (from 1955). I was born and raised, mostly in Economy, a community about five miles northeast of Atkins. Our church in that community was the Sweet Home Free Will Baptist Church.

Born on a hillside in Arkansas
Raised in the country
He was tough
Like his Pa
Said "Sir" to his elders
And "ma'am" to his Ma
A hillbilly boy from Arkansas

Roy
Roy Morris
A boy from Economy

Cleaned a lot of chicken houses
And some barns
Life can be rough
When you work on a farm
Shoveling manure
Won't develop your charms
But it sure will build up
A good set of arms

Roy
Roy Morris
A boy from Economy

Sometime he worked
From sun to sun
'cause he wouldn't stop working
'till the job was done
Twenty-four straight
Is a long hard day
But he toughed it out
'cause he was raised that way

Roy
Roy Morris
A boy from Economy
Hauled a lot of hay
Ten cents a bale
At moving that hay
He could not fail
His fame was spread
Both near and far
If it needed to be done
He'd soon be there

Roy
Roy Morris
A boy from Economy

Joined the Marines
For the Viet-Nam war
Came home once
And went back for more
The scars still hurt
But his heart hurts more
'cause they spat on him
At his country's shore

Roy
Roy Morris
A boy from Economy

Had a lot of different jobs
All through his life
Every day was filled
With trouble and strife
Now he's gone back
To the farm, you see
'cause a country boy
Is all he wants to be

Roy
Roy Morris
A boy from Economy

So he's gone back to doing
What he loves to do
With a tractor and a shovel
And a chain saw, too

When doing farm work
He's having some fun
'cause liking what you do
Is chore number one

Roy
Roy Morris
A boy from Economy

His daughter died
And some nieces, too
When he buried each one
He wished his life was thru
But he kept on doing

What he had to do
'cause you can't just quit
When your family needs you

Roy
Roy Morris
A boy from Economy

Lost his daughter
But he found the Son
When he kneeled at the altar
And gave up the gun
Now the battle for his soul
Has finally been won
Though Satan's work
Is never done

Roy
Roy Morris
A boy from Economy
Roy
Roy Morris
From Sweet Home, Economy

Chapter 73

Beverly Hillbillies

First, Lester Flatt and Earl Scruggs' version

Come and listen to my story about a man named Jed
A poor mountaineer barely kept his family fed
Then one day he was shooting at some food
And up through the ground came a bubbling crude
Oil, that is
Black gold
Texas tea
Well the first thing you know
Old Jed's a millionaire
The kinfolk said
"Jed, move away from there"
They said, "Californy is the place you ought to be"
So they loaded up the truck
And they moved to Beverly
Et cetera, et cetera, et cetera

My version (I don't know why they liked Lester and Earl's version
better than mine)

Approach hither and harken to my fable
Concerning a gentleman with the moniker of Jed

A destitute individual from the hill country
Hardly capable of maintaining adequate nutrition for his relatives
Then one day he shot a hole in the ground
I don't know why he shot a hole in the ground
Because you can't eat dirt, well, actually, I guess you can
Although I don't think it would taste very good
Anyway, I think he was actually shooting at a critter
That they could eat for supper but he missed and
Shot a hole in the ground which is kind of surprising
Because he was supposed to be such a good shot
So, anyway, up through the hole that he shot in the ground
Came a bubbling this gooey, icky-looking black stuff
And he sold it to the oil companies and got rich
But that didn't matter because they still dressed
As if they didn't have a penny to their name
And they still ate road-kill, grits and possum innards
That was kind of dumb, huh!
Y'all come back now, you hear?

Chapter 74

Henderson Mountain

Sung to the tune of "Wolverton Mountain", which is a song about an Arkansas mountain man named Clifton Clowers, who had a pretty, young daughter. I used the melody and the rhythm and made up these new words for the tune one day while I was raking leaves.

This is all there is to the song because I ran out of leaves to rake.

They say don't go on Henderson Mountain
'less you're looking for a fight
'cause old man Dennis is mean as a panther
And he's got an even meaner wife
Her name is Shirley and though she's not burly
She still swings a real mean fist
Even the bears don't mess with Shirley
'cause they don't want to get on her list
Lots of folks have heard me moaning
While I was growing up with that woman
Used to beat me black and blue
It's a wonder I even turned two
If you tangle with that girl
She will knock your head for a whirl
Don't go messing 'round with Shirley
'cause she'll whip you 'till you're squirrel-y
I joined the Marines learned karate too

192

Thought I'd have a chance to win a round or two
But when I got back she still kicked my hiney
'cause while I was gone she learned ju-jitsu
Lots of folks have heard me moaning
While I was growing up with that woman
Used to beat me black and blue
It's a wonder I even turned two
If you tangle with that girl
She will knock your head for a whirl
Don't go messing 'round with Shirley
'cause she'll whip you 'till you're squirrel-y

Chapter 75

John Deere

This is a parody of a song titled "A Dear John Letter", written by Billy Barton during the late part of the Korean War. Lewis Talley first heard Barton sing it when they were both working at the Clover Club in Bakersfield, California. Barton traded the song to Talley for a 1947 Kaiser automobile. Talley actually gave a third of the song back to Barton and sold another third to Fuzzy Owens.

The song was originally recorded for Columbia by Jean Shepard and Terry Preston, a male singer who was using that name because he actually thought his real name sounded made up. The song reached Number One in 1953 and remained on the charts for the better part of a year, receiving both country and pop awards. It assured the solo success of both Jean Shepard and Terry Preston, who began using his own name-Ferlin Husky- again on his next recording.

The song was later re-recorded by Skeeter Davis and Bobby Bare.

I may be mistaken but I seem to recall hearing it sung by Kitty Wells, a LONG time ago.

I think the first part of the real song goes something like this

Dear John
Oh, how I hate to write
Dear John
I must let you know tonight
That my love for you has died

Like fruit upon the vine
And tonight I'll wed another
Dear John

In 1837, John Deere was a pioneer blacksmith in Grand Detour, Illinois when he was challenged by a friend to build a plow that would scour. The cast iron and wood plows from back east were not suitable.

One bright sunny day, when John went to the local sawmill to repair a broken shaft, he saw brilliant sunlight reflected from the surface of a broken saw blade. It was then that he decided that highly polished steel would be perfectly suitable as a plowshare.

He experimented and tested until he got it right.

"I'll never put my name on an implement that hasn't in it the best that is in me", he said.

I wonder how many people know that John Deere was a real person or that he didn't build tractors right from the very start.

John Deere   (continued)

John Deere   John Deere
A blacksmith of renown   Hydraulic lift and forks
John Deere   John Deere
From an Illinois town   Knobby tires get lots of torque
He got started with a plow   Rain and mud or ice and snow
From 1840 until now   Ain't no place it cannot go
A pioneer of agriculture   Though I try not to abuse my
John Deere   John Deere

John Deere   John Deere
Oh, how I love to ride   It's part of family
John Deere   John Deere
Fills my country heart with pride   Really means the world to me
Pulls the baler   Works for hours without rest
Pulls the plow   Makes my farm the very best
I'll make the payments   Couldn't do without my good old
I know, somehow   John Deere
'cause I'll always want to keep my
John Deere

John Deere   John Deere
It loves to cultivate   Not like my beat-up truck
John Deere   John Deere
As a tractor, it's top-rate   On a date, it brings me luck
Closed-in cab, it's really neat   Always let my girlfriend steer
Air conditioned, bucket seat   Four wheel drive, ten forward gears
Stereo and power steering   Oh, she loves to navigate my
John Deere   John Deere

John Deere   John Deere
We work out on the farm   Oh, how I love to ride
John Deere   John Deere
With a special kind of charm   Fills my country heart with pride
To the barn it knows the way   Pulls the baler
With a trailer load of hay   Pulls the plow
And I'll get the crops in with my   I'll make the payments
John Deere   I know, somehow
                                        'cause I'll always want to keep my
                                        John Deere

Chapter 76

My Bologna

This is a song I performed at a company party while I was employed at the Wal-Mart Distribution Center in Clarksville. Management didn't quite appreciate the humor of it as much as my fellow employees did. It's a parody of the Oscar Mayer commercial that was on television a few years ago. (Picture a little kid sitting on a dock at a lake with his fishing pole in one hand and a sandwich in the other).

My Bologna

My bologna has a first name
It's h-o-u-s-e
My bologna has a second name
It's b-r-a-n-d
Oh, I have to eat it every day
And if you ask me why, I'll say
'cause this multi-billion dollar firm
Ain't ever gonna raise my pay

Thicker than Water

Roy Morris

Memorials

Chapter 77

For they shall be comforted

At 4:51 pm on Wednesday, 28 May 1980, my daughter was born at the naval hospital at Camp Kuwae on Okinawa, Japan. Her mother was Cindy Frances Oates. We named her Brandie Lynn.

I had been very apprehensive about becoming a father at the age of 32. I had many foreboding and gloomy fears about the future. I had not been consulted at all regarding the consequences when Cindy decided to become pregnant, or I should say when she made the decision to stop taking precautions to avoid pregnancy. I was bitter, resentful and spiteful, for a long time. I definitely did not appreciate the fact than Cindy had made a decision to become a mother without first checking with me to determine whether or not I wanted to become a father.

My fears were groundless. The most sophisticated genetic research could not have produced a more perfect child. Brandie was beautiful, delightful and sweet. She was a happy child. She was bright-eyed, intelligent and very inquisitive. Rather than being an interruption of my life, she quickly became the focus of my life.

Brandie always became excited when it was time for me to come home from work. What a thrill it was to see her face when I walked through the door. She enjoyed storms and loved to watch the wind and rain of a typhoon while she snuggled, comfortable and warm, in my arms. Our Okinawan neighbors, adults and children alike, adored Brandie and she was delighted at all the attention they gave her.

However, at 11:56 am, on Friday, 29 August 1980, Brandie Lynn died. She had lived on this earth for only 3 months and 1 day. She choked on her formula and died while in the care of our babysitter. It wasn't the sitter's fault. She had three children of her own, so she was very experienced. That dear lady loved our little girl. No, there was no blame placed on her. It just happened. Even grownups have trouble catching their breath when they strangle, so what chance did a baby have?

We took Brandie to Cindy's home in Winchendon, Massachusetts for the funeral and buried her on Saturday afternoon, 6 September 1980. It was a beautiful day, sunny with an occasional small cloud and a cool breeze. During the graveside service, the minister read aloud a short letter I had written the night before as a memorial to my lost love.

After a few weeks, my military duties required me to return to Okinawa. Cindy stayed with her parents. I had read terms like 'the depths of despair' and 'unbearable agony' before but they had been relatively meaningless to me. No longer! I was living on the edge of insanity. I attempted suicide but failed and was given psychiatric treatment. I threw myself into my work. I became like a machine, going through the motions, cold and unfeeling.

In June of 1981, I returned to the United States and was assigned to Camp Lejeune, North Carolina. I found a place to live near the base and went to Massachusetts to pick up Cindy. I was amazed at all the changes she had gone through. She was no longer beautiful, except in my memory. Her face was gaunt and thin with dark circles around her eyes. Her skin, which had been tanned, healthy and smooth, was blotched and sallow. Her hair had lost its shine. Her personality had changed drastically. She was antagonistic toward me. Cindy had become a completely different person

She had apparently never accepted the fact of Brandie's death. I tried to make her see that we had been given a beautiful gift and, even though it had been taken away from us, we could still have a wonderful life together because blood is thicker than water and we belonged to each other as completely as Brandie had belonged to both of us

My arguments served only to infuriate her and my presence brought back all the pain and heartache for her, as fresh and agonizing as if Brandie had just died the day before.

Cindy had a nervous breakdown and went into hysterics. Her father was sympathetic, but he had to ask me to leave. Although it broke my heart, I walked away. I didn't even ask for a ride to the city. It was the middle of the night and I had many miles to go, but at least nobody could see me cry as I walked along a deserted highway in the dark.

Cindy eventually filed for divorce under grounds of irreconcilable differences. I guess it was actually a gesture of kindness. I have never been allowed to see her again. Not when I took her belongings to her out of our household goods shipment from Okinawa. Not when I went up there to visit Brandie's grave. Never.

Sadness settled down deep inside me. I knew that I would never be truly happy again but I know what Heaven is like because I was allowed to visit there from the 28th of May until the 29th of August 1980. And if I still had rightful ownership of my soul, I would gladly trade it away to relive just one of those happy days with my daughter.

Because of the life I have lived, there is very little hope that I can escape the horrors of eternal damnation. However, I still have hope that I will be given at least a few precious moments of time to spend with my darling daughter before I go to my final punishment.

I mourn for my little girl and I have faith that I will see her again, if only for a short time because the Gospel according to Matthew, Chapter 5, Verse 4, quotes my Saviour, Jesus Christ, saying, "Blessed are those who mourn…for they shall be comforted".

Chapter 78

Father's Day

For the first time in my life, during June 1989, I was without my father on Father's Day. Actually, I had been absent from him many times and, in fact, during the past few years, I had rarely been able to visit with him but I always knew he was available where I could get to him, if necessary.

Although my visits with my father were few and far-between, those times I spent with him were precious to me. Sometimes, we hardly talked at all. Just sitting together at the kitchen table seemed enough. But he had a good voice and I can hear him as clearly as if he were speaking to me right now. I don't know if his voice changed over the years. He always sounded the same to me.

One year, at Christmastime, I was sitting with him in his car--I had taken a gift to him and we were just talking about the 'good old days' when I was just a kid. Finally, I said, "You know, Dad, I love you". He was silent for a few moments. Then he said, "Well, son, that goes the same for me". That is as close as he ever came to telling me he loved me. But it's okay because he had expressed his love for me in a thousand different ways over the years, with other words, with his actions, with the way he always treated me.

Dad would always shake my hand when I would first arrive on one of my visits. And we would shake hands again when it was time for me to go. For my dad, a handshake was a precious thing, not to be given lightly. Dad's handshake was better than a signature on a contract. If

Dad shook hands on a deal, that deal was written in stone because he had given his hand on it. And his word.

I remember one of the first times I ever let my father down. I couldn't have been more than nine years old. I was trying to help Dad cut wood with a two-man crosscut saw. For anyone who may not know, a crosscut saw is about five feet long, made of springy steel with a serrated edge. It has handles on each end and is used for sawing through large logs and other oversized pieces of wood. Each man, in turn, must pull the saw across the log in order to cut through it. The man at the opposite end cannot help his partner by pushing against the saw because it will bend in the middle and bind up instead of cutting. Maybe that's where the old expression, 'pulling your own weight' came from.

Anyway, I was pretty small and my hands could barely grip the handle of the saw so this was quite a chore I had before me. It wasn't long before I was tired of pulling that saw. My shoulders were on fire with pain, my back was killing me, blisters had appeared in the palms of my hands, the bugs were flying around my head, and it seemed as if we would never finish sawing even the first block off of that log.

There was a huge pile of sawdust on Dad's side of the log and a very tiny pile on my side, which meant that Dad was doing most of the cutting on his pulls and I was doing hardly any cutting at all on my pulls. My whole body was aching and there were tears in my eyes but my tears were not the result of my physical discomfort. It was very obvious to me that I was letting my father down, that I was not 'pulling my own weight' like I should be. I don't know if Dad noticed my tears. He didn't say anything, if he did. He may have thought I was crying because my blisters hurt and he didn't want to embarrass me. But those were tears of frustration because I wanted to do more, to be more of a helper, to be a better working partner for my Dad. But I wasn't man enough.

I have let Dad down a million times, since then. We have argued. I have ignored and defied him. I have turned away from his leadership and guidance when the advice he gave didn't match what I wanted to hear. I have neglected him and failed to help him on those rare occasions when he needed my help. And through it all, he has loved me.

When I went home for his funeral, I was the one child who had the easiest time coping with it. E. Ray had been dealing with Dad's illnesses and debilitations for a long time.

Shirley and Steve Junior were at the hospital when he died while Robert and Danny had to be with Mom during the entire period.

I didn't live close to home, so I didn't have to watch Dad die little by little, every day. I didn't have to talk with doctors and nurses. I didn't have to make those frequent trips to the hospital, feeling helpless and out of place. I didn't have to make arrangements for the funeral or talk to the minister. All I had to do was show up.

A great many of the people at Dad's visitation and funeral were very old people and that somehow surprised me because I never thought of Dad as being old enough to be acquainted with so many old people. I guess that is normal.

Being home for Dad's funeral had mixed blessings for me. So many of Dad's friends remembered me as a teenager, when I had worked with him in their fields, on their farms or at their sawmills. They told me stories about Dad and reminded me of events in my youth that I had long-since forgotten. I saw a lot of relatives that I hadn't seen for more than ten years. I was able to spend time with people who are important to me. I caught up on some much-needed rest. I even had time to horse around with my younger brothers in the back yard, sparring, shooting baskets and just visiting.

But there was one thing I could not do. I could not allow my gaze to linger on the spot where Dad used to sit and watch us while we played. He would take a kitchen chair and sit about halfway between a huge tree and the corner of a shed. He would usually turn the chair around backward so he could fold his arms over the top of the chair's back. Then, he would sit there, sipping from a large glass of iced tea, talking with us, watching us. Occasionally, he would smoke a cigarette that he would roll for himself from a can of Prince Albert tobacco.

Anyway, I avoided looking at that spot. Dad's spot. A spot in my life, in my heart and in my mind that will forever be an empty space since he is no longer here to fill it.

Father's Day. I miss you, Dad, and........I love you.

Chapter 79

Who cries for Jessica

I'm the one…the one who cries…who cries for Jessica. She was my niece, my bowling buddy, my constant companion, my sweetheart, my special little angel. Some people think she was just a replacement in my heart for my own daughter, who had died at the age of 3 months and 1 day in 1980. That is not true. Jessica was not a replacement. She was her own person, with her own unique personality.

During 1998, I was living with my brother, Robert and his wife, Rosa. I had given up my apartment and moved in with them so I would be able to provide more financial help to them. Cutting down on my personal expenses helped make that possible.

Their oldest daughter, Diana, slept in their bedroom at the front end of their mobile home and Jessica slept in my bedroom at the back end. In order to make the room safer for her, I had put down a thick carpet. We couldn't afford a crib so I put her mattress on the floor. I didn't want to take any chances of having her moving around in her sleep and getting stuck somewhere under my bed, so I put my mattress on the floor right next to hers. That way, she was at arm's length. I could make sure she kept the covers over her. I could reach her at a moment's notice. Her comfort and safety were very important to me. For some reason, I always had the feeling that she needed extra attention, extra care.

Somehow, in some way I can't define, I felt that Jessica NEEDED me so much more than any other child ever had.

After I moved in with Robert and Rosa, I just sort of took over the responsibility for Jessica. Whenever I was not at work, she was with me. In the mornings, while I was getting ready for work, she would act as if she knew that I would soon be leaving and it would seem as if she was trying to ask me not to go.

When I'd leave for work, I'd take Jessica and put her in bed with her parents (my work hours started earlier than Robert's). I'd make sure that at least one of them was awake and knew that Jessica was there. I always settled her in with a fresh bottle of formula and a clean diaper, so she would be comfortable. And I always hated to leaver her.

On Wednesday evenings, Robert and Rosa would usually go out for pizza with our brother, Danny and Mom. Jessica (and sometimes Diana) would go with me to the bowling alley, where I was a member of a Wednesday night league. Robert and Rosa would pick up the kids there when they left the pizza place. Jessica was always popular with the folks at the bowling alley because she had a smile that could melt the hearts of Ebenezer Scrooge and W. C. Fields. And she loved the attention.

I didn't like having Jessica left alone, not even for a minute. I recall a few times when I would come in from working late. Robert, Rosa and Diana would be in the living room and kitchen area. They usually would have already put Jessica to bed. Immediately, I'd go back there to check on her. If she was awake, I would bring her out and get her mixed in with the family. If she was asleep, I would stay back there with her and either read or watch a television program. Just so she wouldn't be alone.

On Thursday morning, the 3rd of December 1998, Robert was already up when I was ready to leave. I reluctantly handed Jessica to him and said, "Now, remember, don't put her back there by herself". I had said those words to him or to Rosa dozens of times.

I was worried about her getting tangled up in the covers, or pulling something down on top of herself or trying to come down the hallway and getting hurt. I know they both probably thought I was being paranoid. And I know they ignored my advice after I was gone. I suppose they thought it was like those old standard warnings people always give, like: 'don't run with a stick, you might fall and put your eye out', or 'don't go swimming right after eating, you might get a cramp and drown'. But that wasn't what I was trying to say. It wasn't that I had precognition or anything like that. There was nothing psychic about it. It was just a "feeling" I always had---don't leave Jessica alone.

That morning at work was like any other. At the time, I was working in the parts department of Diamond International Trucks in Russellville. It's a diesel repair shop and truck sales outlet. My brother-in-law, Dennis, was the repair shop foreman and brother Dan worked in the shop. Shortly before lunchtime, I was called to the phone. When I took the call, I heard Rosa say, "Get down here. Jessica's dead".

I put the phone down and recoiled in horror. I remember shouting to my boss that I had to go. I passed Dennis in the hall. I was already crying and I must have been almost incoherent at the time because he had to follow me all the way out into the parking lot before he was able to figure out what I was saying. It must have been beyond belief for him when he finally understood what I was trying to tell him.

I remember only parts of the trip to Atkins. I don't know how my old truck survived the trip without having the motor explode. I was as close to the edge of insanity as I have ever been, before.

My mind was screaming, and I guess my mouth was, too. It seemed as though I was off to the side somewhere, watching myself, recognizing the signs of my hysteria. With one breath, I would be cursing God for taking her away. With the next breath, I would be pleading with Him to take me instead, to let me die in her place. But God was either not listening or He was not willing to make a deal. That's something for which I will never forgive Him.

Somewhere along the interstate, I realized that an ambulance passed on the other side of the road, heading toward Russellville, with its lights flashing and siren howling. For some reason, that gave me just the smallest measure of hope. I knew Jessica was in there and I thought they wouldn't be in such a hurry if she was really already dead. If they got her to the hospital in time, the doctors could save her.

My hope didn't last long. When I turned in at the trailer, I hit the light pole at the end of the driveway. The mark is there, still. But I was met in the driveway by a woman who told me I had to be strong, that Robert and Rosa would need me to be strong for them. She had destroyed my last hope. I sank to the ground. She didn't realize, of course, that Jessica's parents didn't need ME to be strong for THEM. I needed THEM to be strong for ME. They had lost a daughter but I had lost my special little angel.

I went to get Rosa's mother, Caren, so we could go to the hospital. When I drove up to the house, she was already getting her purse. She has a way of knowing things and this time, she knew that something was terribly wrong. I had to break the news to her.

When we got to the hospital, we were allowed to go into the room where Jessica was. She was covered to the shoulders with a sheet. She was so tiny and still. I brushed her hair. I kissed her face. I cried. Again, I begged God to give life back to her, to let her breathe, to let her open her eyes, to see me and know that I was there. After every absence, her face would instantly light up at her first sight of me and she would always give me her sweetest smile. I needed to have her light shining on me just one more time. I needed to see her smile. But God still wasn't listening. He wouldn't let me have that smile. I would have traded my soul for it.

Very early on Friday morning, I went to the cemetery in Rover to dig her grave. We couldn't afford to hire a professional gravedigger so it was up to me. I borrowed picks and shovels and threw them into the back of my truck. Somewhere along the road, I was stopped by the police because of my erratic driving. At first, the officer thought I was on drugs or drinking, or even mentally disturbed but after I was finally able to explain what my mission was, I was allowed to proceed.

It was a rainy day but at least, that made the digging easier than it had been the last time I had dug a grave up there and I had borrowed a better set of tools, this time. It was very late when I finished, although some help had arrived later in the day. I would cry for a while, then I would go back to swinging that pick or hoisting that shovel. It was 'way past dark when I gave up digging. There was no moon that night so I couldn't see what I was doing as well as I could, the time before.

Before dawn on Saturday, the 5th of December 1998, I went back to the cemetery to finish digging the grave. I took a bucket with me to bail out the water that had collected overnight. I dug deeper and squared off the corners of the grave.

Then, I went back to Atkins and got cleaned up so I could go to the funeral home for the visitation. Carl Rackley had literally performed miracles since the time of Jessica's death, bringing her back from the medical examiner's office in Little Rock, clothing her in such a way that the autopsy scars wouldn't show, obtaining a proper casket......

Brother Danny had performed miracles, too. He got a personal loan at the bank to pay for the funeral expenses, made the arrangements for the visitation and the funeral, took care of family business.....

Compared to everything else that was done, my part was simple. All I had to do was dig a hole in the dirt. But it was a job that I was very nearly incapable of doing because it was a hole where an important part of my life would be buried away from me forever.

Somehow, I got through the visitation. Family, friends and well-wishers arrived. Everyone expressed concern and pity for the parents' loss. Very few people understood the extent of MY loss. Very few people realized she was MY special little angel and God hadn't allowed her to live on this earth even for eleven full months.

I don't know if there was an organized convoy from the funeral home in Atkins to the cemetery in Rover. I had to leave there a little early so I would have time to bail water out of the grave, again. I didn't want to set Jessica's casket down in the water.

There was to be a graveside service. When Carl arrived in the hearse with Jessica, I broke down all over again. There was a tent. There were chairs for the family. There was a platform for Jessica's tiny casket.

When everything was ready, I was the last to take my seat. The minister was not going to start the service without having me in my proper place. I didn't want to sit down. By doing so, I would be giving my permission, the final permission, for Jessica to be forever separated from us. I had no choice. I took my place. The service, the words, the music.

It seemed as though my heart was being torn out. My special little angel would be gone and I would be alone, again. I was the last to touch her face before the casket was closed. A metal cover was clamped over the casket. Carl had explained to me that the hood would help keep the water from rising over and flooding the casket. That was a bit of comfort to me.

I got down into the grave. When the casket was handed down to me, Carl said, softly, "Don't drop her, Roy". I replied, "I never have, sir". After I positioned the casket, I fell to my knees and put my arms over it with my face pressed against it. It was such a tiny thing. I told her that I loved her and that I would miss her, forever.

I reached for my shovel. The dirt had a lot of shale and rock so Carl had cautioned me to cover the top of the casket slowly and carefully so there wouldn't be any loud rattling noises. He was helping me to know the correct way of putting my angel to bed for the last time and I was grateful.

After I covered the top of the casket, I climbed out and started filling around the sides. With every shovelful, I was widening the gap that would separate Jessica from me for the rest of my life. Soon, I could not continue. I sank to my knees, crying.

Others took over the task. They were strong and efficient. I tried to tell them to slow down. She had died too soon. Her life had been too short. And now, her burial was progressing too rapidly. Eventually, however, it was all over and we slowly departed, leaving her body in the ground and her soul in the lap of Jesus.

I cry for Jessica on 12 January because that was her birthday. I cry on the anniversary of her death. I cry while I'm alone at work, clearing a pasture, gathering eggs, repairing a fence, cutting firewood or cutting grass. I cry in the morning because I didn't get enough mornings to share with her. I cry in the evening because she isn't here to play with, to read to, to tuck into bed. I cry at night when I dream of having to bury her.

I'm the one..........the one who cries......who cries for Jessica.

Chapter 80

Mom

11 April 2004

Some random thoughts about Alta Laverne Morris....our Mom.

By today's standards, she would have been accused of child endangerment because she raised us in houses that had no plumbing.

By today's standards, she would have been accused of child endangerment because she raised us in houses that had no electricity.

In fact, sometimes, she raised us in places where there was no house at all.

But I don't remember feeling endangered...and we did get raised, sure enough, after all.

She made water gravy and biscuits for breakfast, for supper she cooked beans, taters and biscuits. Sometimes, there wasn't much to go around but she never dipped anything into her plate until after every child had a plateful, first.

But there were occasional special treats. In the summertime, a huge watermelon would be sliced and shared. In the wintertime, she would use a little vanilla extract and a cup of sugar to turn a dishpan full of snow into the most delicious snow ice cream.

I'm not saying she was anything extra special. She was just a simple country woman who tried to take care of her family the best she could.

With a hug for little shoulders that needed reassurance or comfort, with a kiss for little elbows and knees that needed healing, with a hickory switch for little bottoms that needed tanning…..she raised us.

From the tip of the Alaskan peninsula to the peak of Mount Fuji in Japan, from the shores of Okinawa to the jungles and rice paddies of Viet-Nam, whenever I thought about home, I thought about Mom.

Because wherever Mom was…..that was home!

Chapter 81

Rest In Peace

16 July 2006

James Ezell Johnston truly does rest in peace. We know this for two reasons.

First and foremost, he was a "saved" man. The blood of Jesus had ensured a place in Glory for him. His soul was washed in the Blood.

The second reason is equally important. In many different scriptures, the Bible says that we will be judged according to our deeds. Ezell's deeds speak for themselves. He lived his life the way a REAL man should.

No man has ever said that Ezell treated him unfairly, either personally or in business.

Ezell would not--WOULD NOT--speak a lie. And I never heard him speak unkindly about any person.

Ezell would help anybody who needed help--no matter what. I have seen him put himself out so MANY times to lend a helping hand. To strangers as well as to neighbors.

Ezell was a hard-working man. Many times, I've been in the hay fields with him and I was constantly amazed at his strength, at his knowledge of the land and of the farm and at his expertise in handling equipment and livestock.

One of my earliest memories of Ezell was when I went out to cut firewood with him when my Dad was "laid up" from a sawmill injury and couldn't go out to do the wood-cutting for our family. Ezell made sure I received half of the firewood even though I was too small to do even a third of the work.

I grew up with Ezell's two oldest sons, Lavon and Larry, and I'm proud to say they are my life-long best friends.

Ezell was a second father to me. I slept under his roof countless times and ate many a meal at his table. I could tell a thousand stories about him…and they would all be GOOD stories, much to his credit.

While I was visiting with Larry after Ezell's death, Larry said, "Well, he's gone on to Glory". To that, I can only say, "AMEN".

Chapter 82

Papa Troy

30 September 2006

Alongside my Dad, I worked many a day at Troy Ennis' sawmill, running strips and slabs and stacking lumber. Alongside Troy's two oldest sons, Larry and Leon, I hauled count-less bales of hay behind Troy's baler. During my youth, I was befriended by Troy (and by the entire Ennis Family) so many times, in fact, any time and every time I needed a friend.

So I considered it a PRIVILEGE and an HONOR to be chosen by the Ennis Family to be the church member who would read the following poem during a service at the Sweet Home Free Will Baptist Church in Economy--a poem written by a member of the Ennis Family--a poem that none of them would have been able to read through tear-filled eyes.

Remembering Papa Troy

It's been four years since we've seen your face
But we all feel your presence in this place
The little white church--that you loved so
Is where your children found the Lord--and go
A saw miller man with a heart of gold

With a love for his Lord and family so bold
Always with a twinkle in those eyes of blue
So deeply he loved all that he knew
Your legacy lives on in the faces of seven
Each boy and girl knowing their Dad is in Heaven
An honor it is to have your last name
As we all work hard to bring it no shame
God called your name the last of September
It is a day each one will always remember
With broken hearts and tear-filled eyes
We held each other to say our goodbyes
Stories were told and memories shared
So many came to show how they cared
You had worked so hard for this final payday
Your life's testimony gave the preachers plenty to say
Days have passed and we still miss you so
As on life's journey we continue to go
Remembering your smile and how happy you would be
If but for a moment--your Sweet Home to see

Jan Ennis

Chapter 83

Few and Far Between

7 May 2008

If you live long enough, you're eventually going to have to say goodbye to a lot of people who are near and dear to your heart and, no matter how many times it happens, it never gets any easier.

Saying goodbye to Ms Wilma Johnston was the next worst thing to saying goodbye to my own mother. I spent a major part of my youth with her two oldest sons, Lavon and Larry, and I was made welcome and comfortable in the Johnston home.

I guess my favorite memories of Ms Wilma involve eating thousands of meals at her table. Evening meals were always good but my personal favorite was always breakfast.

The best breakfast in the world for an Arkansas boy is biscuits and gravy and Ms Wilma's biscuits and gravy were as good as my own Mom's were.

And I have to admit that Lavon, Larry and I were spoiled rotten because we never had to question our right to have such wonderful food placed before us. We never had to think about what sacrifices she had to make in order to have breakfast ready when we got out of bed on the nights that I stayed over. She was never too sick to cook, no matter how sick she might really have been. Even on Mother's Day, she never had the luxury of just "sleeping in". Like my own Mom, Ms Wilma started every day--EVERY day--doing her best to take care of her family. Mothers like those two are few and far between.

If you're thinking, by now, that her cooking was the only thing I appreciate about Ms Wilma, then you would be mistaken. I'm just trying to point out that a person doesn't really become truly memorable by any one single act or deed.

A really remarkable thing about Ms Wilma is that she did all of the things that good mothers do...and she did them thousands upon thousands of times, through the years. She did them consistently and she did them well, without complaining and, regrettably, with very little show of appreciation from us kids--at least, not while we were still kids.

There were four very important women in my life, from the time I was born until I got married. They were Mom, sister Shirley, neighbor Wanda Jean Ennis, and Ms Wilma.

They all took turns "mothering" me for so many years. And it shames me to say that, during most of those years, I took them all for granted. I said goodbye to Mom in 2004.

In 2008, I said goodbye to Ms Wilma. If I ever have to say goodbye again to anybody who is important to me, I hope it's because I'm the one who leaves. I hope, Ms Wilma, you can somehow hear these words:

Thanks, Ms Wilma, for allowing me to share in the life of your family.

Thanks, Ms Wilma, for the help, guidance and support you gave me.

Thanks, Ms Wilma, for the biscuits and gravy.

Chapter 84

Who still watches over me

On 23 April 2013, it was 24 years since Dad died. Having been born on 7 December 1919, he was 69 years, 4 months, 2 weeks and 2 days of age when he passed away.

He always did the best he could to take care of his family. He treated each one of his children special, although he gave me a lot of whippings during my early years. But I have to admit each of those whippings was well deserved. And if the truth be known, I actually earned a lot more whippings than I ever received.

I was always the black sheep of the family and I brought shame upon his name more times than could ever possibly be counted. But he never stopped loving me, just the same as the rest. I'll never stop wondering how he managed to do that. It's just beyond my ability to understand.

It's not that I was a mean or vicious kid. I never got into a fight at school unless I was defending somebody against one of the school bullies. The bad guys learned to be afraid of me but the other kids never had any reason to be. So, no, I wasn't actually evil but I made a lot of mistakes. Doing the wrong thing always seemed to come naturally to me.

Some folks believe in Guardian Angels who help them avoid bad situations or help them keep from making mistakes. So many times, it seemed as though I had a Guardian Demon, whose sole purpose was to ensure that I always took the wrong course of action.

No matter what I did, it turned out to be the wrong thing to have done. No matter how many facts I had on which to base a decision, there was always one small fact that got overlooked which made my decision ultimately the wrong choice. Regardless of the situation.

And it wasn't always just me, it wasn't always something that I did or said that turned out so wrong. It wasn't always my fault. Bad things happened when I was around. Tires went flat, fuel tanks ran dry, car engines died, machinery failed, farm equipment broke down. Stuff that I had not even TOUCHED. It just happened because I was there.

All things considered, I might be said to have been living a cursed life. During most of my miserable existence, I have considered the possibility that I might be nothing more than an experiment that God is conducting, just to see how much trouble and misery one person can take before just giving up.

Of all the Morris children, I was the least deserving of a father's love. But I received it, anyway. Go figure. How can I compute the worth, the value of something like that? For 41-plus years, he did whatever he could to help me get along, to help me be more of a success, to help me survive.

When Dad died, it was logical to assume that all of that was at an end. There was no longer anything he could do for me. Or so I believed. Wrong! Dad had left a legacy that provided a cushion for me, even after he was gone. Everybody that had known Dad knew that he was "one of the good guys". Everybody that had known him was willing to give me an occasional "helping hand". I was worthy of assistance, simply because I was one of Steve Morris' kids.

I could buy groceries on credit. I could get medicine on credit at Haney's Pharmacy.

I bought several used cars, at one time or another, with little or no money down and with very reasonable payments (with no interest or service charge). I was able to get my vehicles worked on and didn't have to pay the full price all at once for parts and labor.

After I came home the last time, I was given plenty of odd jobs by folks in and around Economy and by folks down in the Atkins "bottoms" because I was one of Steve Morris' kids. Even though Dad was gone.

In my youth, I had worked for many various farmers around Pope County but mostly for the Burnetts, the Ennises and the Johnstons in the

Economy neighborhood. After I was home to stay, I did considerable part-time work on the Johnston farm. One of the main reasons I was able to work for Gerald and Charlotte Johnston was because Gerald (and his father, Finis) had been friends with Dad for decades.

Back in Gerald's younger days, he and Dad worked together a lot. They did some hay hauling, some sawmilling, some fence building and they shoveled a LOT of manure out of various chicken houses and barns. Before I came along and got big enough to start doing my share of the work, Dad worked with my older brother, E. Ray, with a young fellow named Jackie Dale Duvall…and with Gerald Johnston. They all shared many a jug of sweet iced tea and cold bologna sandwiches while sitting on the back of an old hay wagon or pickup truck.

Dad treated all those boys the same--like sons. And Gerald has always had a lot of respect, admiration and love for Dad. That's why I was hired to do those jobs on the farm for Gerald and Charlotte. Because Dad had already paved the way for me, all those long years ago.

I reckon I was about 60 years old when Gerald asked me how long I had to go before I would be eligible for social security, when I could at least semi-retire. I figured it up and told him I would turn 62 in October of 2009. Then he said, "Well, if you want to work full-time on the farm, I'll keep you employed until you can draw social security". It was a good deal, so I agreed. Over the years I had done all sorts of jobs on the farm, such as building, repairing and painting fences, helping to renovate a couple of the farm houses, raking and hauling hay, repairing roofs on chicken houses and barns, bush hogging, spraying poison on weeds and briars, clearing fence rows, helping with the chickens and cattle and doing all sorts of miscellaneous projects. I stayed busy and it was work I liked.

In December 2008, Gerald and Charlotte decided to lease out the farm and all of the farm equipment. However, he remembered that he had told me that he would keep me employed until I became eligible for social security. At that time, I had 10 months to go before I would turn 62. When they came down from Springdale at Christmastime, Gerald drove out to see me and tell me his plans for the farm. Then he told me about his plans for me. He said that, as of that moment, I was officially semi-retired. Then he handed me a Christmas card with a Christmas bonus check inside. And he told me that, on the first of each month, he would send me a retirement check until I started drawing my social security. In return, I could do yard work around a couple of the houses on the farm.

He didn't have to do that. It wasn't something I expected, or really had any reason to expect. But that's the way he interpreted the offer of job security he had promised me when he hired me on fulltime. You see, a person like that, well, his word is important to him and that's the method he chose to keep his word. He made that original offer to me, in the first place, because of Dad. And that's the way he kept his word, in the second place, again because of Dad.

I should add, right here, that I live in one of the houses on the Johnston Farm. I've lived on the farm for several years, now. This is another way that Gerald has found to honor Dad's memory. This has saved me hundreds of dollars each month. In addition to everything else, Gerald is the one who is financing the initial printing of this book, which is another expense which might never be repaid if there aren't enough buyers for the finished product.

I might add, further, that Dad left the same kind of lasting impression on the Morris children that he left on everybody else who knew him. When I first got out of the Marine Corps and came home to stay forever (the first time), I lived in the upstairs portion of Robert's and Dan's house (where they had Mom living with them). When I came home to stay forever (the second time), Shirley and Dennis gave me a place to stay. When I came home to stay forever (the third time), E. Ray and Jannie let me live in a house on their property. When I came home to stay forever (the last time), Shirley and Dennis took a house that they owned in the Dover area and had it moved to a spot of land owned by Steve Junior and his wife, Polly, in the Economy community. They set it up, plumbed it and had it wired for electricity. To be more specific, they did all that work themselves, with a lot of help from Junior and with a little help from me. I'm considered (by some) to be reasonably smart but I'm not much of a plumber or electrician. I did a lot of work but I had to be told everything that needed to be done. I lived in Shirley's house on Junior's land for quite a few years. But that's the way the Morris family does things. That's the way Mom and Dad raised their children to be. I'd have to win the lottery to ever be able to pay back just my family for all the help they have given me, not to mention all the other people to whom I owe so much.

But if it weren't for Dad being the kind of person he was while he was alive, then all of the people who helped me during the first 41 years of my life might not have helped me. And if people didn't have good memories of Dad after he died, then all of the people who have helped me during the past 20-odd years of my life might not have done so.

Therefore, during my entire life, it has been my father that I've had to thank for a lot of the good things in my life. Even dying didn't stop him from helping me. If anything, his death made him even stronger. So, although he has been gone for about the last one-third of my life so far, he is still the one who watches over me.

Thanks, Dad.

Thicker Than Water

Roy Morris

And Furthermore

Chapter 85

Why am I still here?

When I was 11 years old, a witch told me that my life would end at the age of 35. She lived at the top of the hill on Burnett Cove Road in the Economy community a few miles northeast of Atkins. She was related, in some way, to a man named Golden Holmes, one of our neighbors. Perhaps she was his mother. She was exceedingly old. I don't think I ever knew her name.

Mister Holmes worked with Dad from time to time, at various sawmills, in the hay fields, cleaning out chicken houses or at other odd jobs. I recall that they both worked for the company that tore down the old two-story school building in Atkins.

Mister Holmes had two children. The boy, Carl, was roughly the same age as E. Ray and the girl, Geneva, was about the same age as Shirley. For a period of time, our family lived at the bottom of the hill near the junction of Burnett Cove Road and highway 247, which was nothing more than a dirt road, at the time, so our families visited back and forth quite often. Carl and Geneva would run around with E. Ray and Shirley and we would often go swimming or to the movies together.

But….that old lady. She was nice but it was very unsettling for me to spend very much time around her. She had a way of looking at me that made me feel as is she was looking into my soul. Sometimes, when I was near her, I would feel a cold chill come over me and it would seem as if the rest of the people around us would fade into a sort of gray area and we would be the only two people in focus. They would still be there but they would be apart from us.

When I was younger, I had a lot of warts on my hands and fingers. She took them off. I mean, she made them go away. She noticed that, when I would put my hands into my pockets, I would sometimes scrape a couple of the warts and that hurt.

One day, she called me to her side. She looked closely at my hands and carefully counted the warts. Then, she took her finger and drew circles around each wart while she was mumbling something so lowly that I couldn't hear what she was saying. Those warts dried up and peeled off within a couple of weeks. None of them ever came back.

I never forgot the things she told me. She told me a lot about my future. Things that came to pass. Not just specific events, either. She predicted the circumstances and even the emotions and feelings that would precede or follow those events. Those happenings are not part of the story at this time. I just want to stress that there were enough correct predictions to assure me that she knew what she was talking about, so when she told me that my life would end at the age of 35, I went through my life believing, with a fairly significant amount of confidence, that my life actually would end, as she had foretold.

Some of the folks who knew me well during my youth would probably be willing and able to verify that I lived life at a pace that was just a little faster than normal. I truly did march to the beat of a different drummer. I sincerely thought that I didn't have a lot of time so I had to cram a lot of stuff into the time I had.

Not that I was reckless or foolhardy, although I did a lot of dumb things, the same as any young fellow might do. But I was driven by forces that other people weren't even aware of. I had an insatiable need to be better, faster, stronger, to do more, to be more, to leave more of a mark because I had less time than other folks had to get it all done.

Even though I say it, myself, I became somewhat of a local legend in many ways. I did all sorts of farm labor. I was the top hay hauler in the county, possibly in the state. My feats of strength and agility were discussed around the stove at the old neighborhood store. I had a set of weights (barbells and dumbbells) that was the envy of my friends. As a jogger, I could beat the school bus from the school in Atkins to our home in Economy.

That drive to excel, to achieve, to DO, before time ran out was part of the reason why I joined the Marines, took up boxing, wrestling and karate, volunteered for duty in Viet-Nam twice, went as high as the rank of Gunnery Sergeant (E-7) in the enlisted ranks and then became a Marine officer. I wanted to be a Leader and I had to hurry.

On 9 October 1982, I turned 35. I believed it would be the last year of my life but I didn't know whether I had 1 more day or 364 more days. At that time, I was stationed in Camp Lejeune, North Carolina. I had remarried to a wonderful girl, Linda, and had a darling 10-year old stepdaughter, Carla. I was assigned as Officer In Charge, Storage Section, Marine Corps Base with three junior officers and 215 enlisted Marines working for me. I was simultaneously serving as a Platoon Commander with 45 Marines in my platoon. I was also the Company Training Officer for General Military Subjects and was the Company Physical Fitness Officer. I was very busy but I was also very happy. At least, I would have been happy if I had not been convinced that I was living out my last days. The cloud of doom that had followed me since I was 11 years old was coming overhead and the darkness was closing in fast.

I had many arguments with my boss, a Lieutenant Colonel. We argued regarding warehousing and storage procedures, regarding the promotion policies for the junior Marines in the command, regarding the standards of professionalism we should be able to expect from our Staff Non-Commissioned Officers. We argued simply because I was reluctant to attend "Officer's Call" when he wanted "Officer's Call" to be staged after hours at the Officers Club (where he could have a few drinks while having informal discussions with all of the Section Leaders) instead of having "Officer's Call" in the conference room at our place of business.

I won most of our arguments because I was right. I was a lowly Chief Warrant Officer (the equivalent of a Captain) and I would not have argued with a Lieutenant Colonel if I hadn't already known that I was right. I can be very uncompromising when I know I'm right but he could be uncompromising, too, even when he was proven wrong. Especially when he was proven wrong. And he could definitely hold a grudge. He found reasons to charge me with Conduct Unbecoming to an Officer and sent me before a court martial.

I resigned in disgust and was honorably discharged.

I had been the best Marine and the best Marine officer that anybody could have been. At every command, I had repeatedly been assigned as a Platoon Commander, and at every command, my platoon was the best platoon, winning the "honors" at many competitions in many different categories because I always trained my platoon to be the best. I was the best leader, the best instructor, the highest scorer on the rifle and pistol ranges, the highest scorer on the physical fitness test, the best at so MANY things. I was considered, by peers and seniors alike, to be the quintessential Marine Leader. But my Marine live was over.

After I was no longer a Marine Officer and Gentleman, Linda divorced me and kicked me out of the house, ending our married life.

So, there I was. My married life was over. My professional life was over. My life had ended at the age of 35, as predicted. My only problem was that I hadn't died. How was I supposed to go on? Where was I supposed to go? What was I supposed to do?

I came home. I packed my few clothes in my old car---Linda got the other newer car. And the house. And everything else. By the time I crossed the Arkansas line, it was late in the day on 8 October 1983. A little after midnight, I reached Russellville.

So it was officially my birthday, the 9th of October. By some standards, I would now be considered to be 36 and my final year of trying to exist with a sword hanging over my head was now presumably over.

However, I had never considered it to be my actual birthday until 6:00 pm on the 9th because that was my birth hour. So, by my reckoning, I was not in the clear for almost another 18 hours. If I could make it past 6:00 pm, then there would be no telling how much more time I might have because I would have survived the old lady's prediction. At least, in a manner of speaking.

I exited from Interstate 40, drove over to Highway 64, turned west, drove past the old Firestone Plant and turned left onto Elmira. I was just a few blocks away from E. Ray and Jannie's house, where I would be staying temporarily in a house on their property.

As I crossed the railroad tracks, an oncoming train clipped the rear bumper of my car, knocking it sideways but also knocking it out of the way of the rest of the train. Back in those days, there was no barrier that dropped at the crossing, but the lights had been flashing and the bell had been clanging. I had been so exhausted from driving straight through from North Carolina that I almost died on 9 October 1983, just a few hours from getting clear of the prediction.

Of course, she had actually been right about my life ending at the age of 35, as she had been right about so MANY things through the years. My personal life had ended at the age of 35. My professional life had ended at the age of 35. And, if not for split-second timing with less than a fraction of a second to spare, my physical life would have ended under the wheels of that train…at the age of 35.

So now, here I am all these years later. I will turn 66 next month on 9 October 2013 and I have no idea how I have made it this far. And the only question I have--the same question I have been asking myself for more than a quarter of a century is this:

Why am I still here?

Chapter 86

Better Off Dead

I have always known that I will be alone when I die. And I have always known that I will be the cause of my own death. Try as I might, I can't remember a time when I was not aware of these two facts.

There will be plenty of people who will be absolutely convinced that I have gone to Hell because of the way I lived (rather, I should say because of the way they THINK I lived). I'll tell you a little-known secret. I'm not anywhere near to being the evil creature that some people think I am. Granted, I've made a lot of bad decisions…but I've had a lot of bad decisions made FOR me, too.

And there will be some people who will fervently hope and pray that I have gone to Hell. They will have a need to believe that I am suffering eternal torment simply because they just can't stand the thought that I might actually have found some measure of peace. Those people will be the ones who are most aware of my many faults. They will not want to believe any good thing that might be said about me. They will pray against me, hoping that their prayers will help to condemn me.

Also, there will be some people (not many, admittedly) who will be aware of my few redeeming qualities. They will simply not want to believe the bad things that will be said about me. They will pray for me, hoping that their prayers will intercede in my behalf.

Everybody who ever knew me will be absolutely convinced that whatever conclusion they make regarding my destiny is the correct conclusion and nothing will ever change their minds, whether they are pro-Roy or anti-Roy.

But you know what? None of those people have the final decision about where I will be spending eternity. No matter whether they loved me or hated me. It won't make any difference if they want to believe that I found forgiveness or if they want to believe that I have been condemned. None of those people will be in charge of determining my final destiny.

I have to face only one Judge--God. And God already knows everything about me, both the good and the bad. He doesn't have to listen to the people who will be praying for my salvation because He is already aware of everything they could possibly have to say in my favor. But also, He doesn't have to listen to the people who will be praying for my condemnation, either, because He is already aware of everything they could possibly have to say against me.

It will be the very first time that I will have been judged by somebody who has ALL of the facts. That means it will be the first time that I can be assured of receiving perfect justice from an unprejudiced judge. And His decision is not only final, it's everlasting.

Yes, I know there's a chance that the scales of justice may not swing in my favor. My evil deeds may outweigh the good. But I've said the Sinner's Prayer and asked for His forgiveness. I've been baptized, so I know I'll have the very best legal representative (Jesus) speaking in my behalf when I face my judge (God).

Yes, I admit that I go backsliding every day because I am just a weak and imperfect human being, just like anybody else, but I believe that He is willing to take my weakness into consideration. I believe, and that's the bottom line.

If He condemns me, then so be it. I'll go to Hell. However, there is one consolation. The Bible quotes the Savior Jesus saying, "Blessed are those who mourn, for they shall be comforted". I have mourned for my daughter, Brandie Lynn, since 1980 and I have mourned for my niece, Jessica Marie, since 1998. So if I am condemned to Hell, then I believe that God will allow me a few moments of time with my daughter and my niece before He casts me away. That's all I can expect. Jesus said that I would be comforted but He did not say that it would be an everlasting comfort.

You see, God is in charge of Time. He invented Time. All of Time belongs to Him. From the beginning of Time to the end of Time. So

I'm positive that He can spare a few moments of Time for me to spend being comforted by the presence of my daughter and my niece. I am absolutely assured of this because if God doesn't allow it, then that would mean that Jesus lied when He said that I would be comforted, and the Son of God is not capable of lying.

Worst case scenario: If I'm condemned, then I know that I can count on having those few precious moments with Brandie and Jessica. After that, I'll march into Hell with my head held high.

Best case scenario: If I'm not condemned, then I'll get to spend all of eternity in the presence of my daughter and my niece, surrounded by Angels and close to Jesus. THAT would be a comfort worth dying for.

Now, suppose neither of these scenarios happens. What if there is no God, no Heaven or Hell, no Angels or demons, no Satan and no Jesus? What if the Bible is really only a collection of conjectures and wishful thinking? So what? What if there is nothing after death except oblivion? That would be fine with me. I would welcome oblivion because oblivion means that I would no longer suffer from all the pain, heartache and misery that I have endured during the major portion of my life. If there is no God, no reward and no punishment, then oblivion is a pretty attractive alternative. I can readily accept the fact that I would lose my memories of all the good things in my life because that means that I would also finally be rid of my memories of all the bad things in my life. I'm willing to take the good with the bad.

But let's be realistic. There IS a God. I know. I have been in the presence of Angels just as surely as I have been in the presence of demons. I have felt the presence of some forces that were neither of these. And I have witnessed events that would have been totally impossible without the influence of a Supreme Being.

If there were no God, there would be no reason for flowers to smell good, no reason for rainbows to be so beautiful, no reason for leaves to have so many different colors in the fall, no reason for music or poetry to be written, no reason for the seasons to change, no reason for the world to turn, no reason for the universe to exist. If there were no God, there would be no reason for anything at all.

So, yes, there is a God. Jesus lived a real life, died a real death and was resurrected for one special reason--so that He could assume responsibility for all of the sins of all people who live, have lived and all of those yet to live until the end of the earth. None of us can comprehend, or even imagine the strength and the power of such as He. Mortal man has trouble enough with just trying to assume responsibility for his own children, whether there be a dozen or just one or two. How can we relate to someone who has the ability to carry the responsibility for ALL people? The answer, of course, is that we can't.

The only way we can relate to God and His Son is through faith. We have no hope of ever understanding, so we simply have to believe. Yes, it really is just that simple. The Son of God was made mortal so that He could better relate to our problems, our aches and pains, our worries and trials and tribulations. So Jesus knows. He understands and He cares. He has walked a mile in our shoes. Many times over. And He walked the mile up that hill to His destiny, with full knowledge and acceptance of what was to come. THAT mile, none of us could have walked. But He did it so that we would know that He under-stands and that He loves us.

All that He asks of us in return is that we have faith, that we believe. Well, I have started to believe and to have faith. I believe He loves me enough to be able to forgive me for giving up on life. He knows of all my lies--and all of the lies that have been told about me. He knows of all my evil deeds--and all of the evil deeds that have been done to me. He knows of all the pain, misery and heartache I have caused--and all of the pain, misery and heartache I have suffered. He knows that I can't abide with these things much longer and He understands. And I believe that I will find, in death, the peace of mind that, in life, has eluded me for so many decades.

So many things have gone wrong and are still going wrong. So many problems exist. So many bad things are happening to me and around me. I'm not strong enough to with-stand so many burdens. If these conditions continue, I'll be Better Off Dead.

Chapter 87

Not Yet Ready

After I died, I found myself walking with Jesus in the countryside of Pope County, Arkansas, where I had been born and raised. I could not remember the reason for, nor the circumstances, of my own death but that did not bother me at all.

Like a proud child, I was showing Jesus the places where I had played in the woods and meadows, where I had first learned to skim stones over the surface of a pond, where I had first found the nerve to swing on a vine across a ravine, even the tiny stream where I had learned to dogpaddle.

Even though Jesus knew every detail of my childhood better than I could ever hope to remember it, I never got the impression that He was patronizing me or making fun of me by allowing me to show Him these places. Rather, He was simply indulging me the way a loving, caring parent will do for a favored child.

His presence was absolutely overwhelming. While I was with Him, I felt no fear, nor could I imagine anything of which to be afraid. I felt no hunger. Nor did I feel thirst. Indeed, I felt as if I might have just finished one of my favorite meals followed by a long, satisfying drink from a tall glass of very cold, clear water. All of my wants and needs from my mortal existence had been washed away by the fullness of this new existence I was now experiencing with Him.

All the seasons of nature seemed to be occurring simultaneously, as if the best of each was being presented for my personal enjoyment. My senses were alive with the wonders of the earth. Never could my mortal mind have conceived such a kaleidoscope of colors. Those foothills of the Ozark Mountains had never been so beautiful. Each different shade of color was so sharp and clear, so distinct.

My eyesight was so good, I could watch individual leaves as they soaked up moisture of an early morning dew. In vivid detail, I could watch fish in a nearby creek as they chased the water bugs skimming across the surface of the water.

My hearing had improved a thousand fold. I heard the tiny snap of a cone as it broke away from the branch of a distant tree. I discerned the high-pitched chirpings of four tiny robin hatchlings as their mother returned to the nest in a willow tree. I heard the rustling of the grass as baby rabbits left their burrow to explore the world. No manmade music could have been anywhere near as beautiful as the music of nature which I was hearing. The sighing of the wind in the treetops, the gurgling of water as it ran down a small embankment and the sounds of the animals made the most fascinating music possible.

I smelled blackberries as they ripened in the valley. I smelled apple blossoms and honey from a nearby hive inside a dead tree. I distinguished the smell of peach blossoms from across the valley as they mixed with the aroma of oats and wild onions growing in a field. And I smelled the rather sharp odor of pine shavings and the drier, mustier odor of rice hulls, both of which are used in Arkansas as ground coverings inside chicken houses.

My sense of touch was so greatly enhanced that I could feel each point of contact as a caterpillar crawled across the back of my hand. I felt vibrations in the air as a hawk flew overhead and I felt the shock waves in the ground as a rock rolled down a nearby bluff and crashed into other rocks at the bottom.

I pulled the pistil from the stem of a honeysuckle flower and ran it over my tongue, tasting the sweetest nectar imaginable. Grapes from a hanging vine were equally pleasing to my palate and a taste of blackberries from a thicket combined to convince me that nature does, indeed, provide food fit for a king.

Then Jesus spoke. He said, "You have finally attained peace and fulfillment with nature, with the world and with yourself. Now is the time for you to seek the attainment of peace with God and that can only be accomplished through Me, for I am the Way and the Light".

When He spoke, I heard Him not only with my ears, but with every molecule of my body. It seemed as though He was communicating with the very fiber of my being. He was speaking directly to my soul! His was not a loud and booming voice, as you might imagine it sounding through a megaphone, but it had a resonance and quality that carried it across the hills, over the meadow and up the mountainside with undiminished clarity and tone. His voice seemed to emanate from the trees, from the flowers, from the earth with a soft, quiet melody. Every syllable was pronounced very distinctly and clearly. His voice washed over me in waves, leaving me wishing I could spend eternity just standing there relishing the way His voice had sounded to me, had felt to me.

Finally, I found the ability to ask, "Jesus, why have I been allowed to know all these wonders of nature? How did I earn the right to experience such beauty and pleasure?" He replied, "You have been shown the wonders of this world so that you might have the slightest idea of other wonders which are yet to come. As great as these might seem, the wonders of this world are as nothing compared to the wonders of Heaven. Now is the time to establish whether or not you have the right to experience these wonders. It is time to review your life, to determine your worthiness to enter the Kingdom of Heaven".

As He spoke, there appeared in the sky a panoramic vista of the wrongful deeds I had committed during my mortal life. As the visions cleared and as the number of my deeds increased, I realized that my life had been wasted in the pursuit of material things, material pleasures. Too often had I spent my time doing what I wanted to do instead of doing what I should have done. Too often had I given in to the many lures of wickedness. Too often had I sinned. Visions of my sins filled the sky, from horizon to horizon and beyond. And each vision was an indictment of me.

With each additional vision, the sadness in Jesus' face grew ever deeper and with each additional vision, my hope for salvation slowly dimmed until it was completely gone. He turned to me. I knew my time of judgment had come. I could not face Him. He said, "You have committed many sins". Then, an uncontrollable terror filled me. Fear of the unknown became fear of the KNOWN as I became aware of the punishments awaiting me. As I contemplated the horrors that would be my just reward for the wasted life I had led, the icy cold hand of fear gripped my heart like a vise. My pulse pounded in my head. A trembling started deep inside me. My knees grew weak and would not hold me. I fell to the ground at Jesus' feet.

But somehow, I found the courage and the strength to rise again. During my mortal life, I had been lauded, as a military man, for bravery on several occasions. I had faced many formidable obstacles and challenges but it took all the courage I could muster, all the strength I possessed to be able to lift my eyes to the countenance of Jesus Christ.

In His eyes, I saw the terrible sadness that had been caused by my evil deeds. On His face, I saw the pain and suffering He was enduring as a result of my wrongdoing. Jesus had lived a mortal life, too, but He had given up that life, dying an excruciatingly painful death for my sake, so that I might have life everlasting......and I had failed Him.

Gone was the fear of the punishment that would be my fate for my evil deeds. Gone was the fear of the retribution that was waiting for me as the "reward" for my wasted life.

Gone was the feeling of hopelessness and despair. All of these were replaced by a deep and sincere regret for having brought sadness to those eyes, regret for the disappointment and pain etched on that face by my miserable, worthless life, regret for having failed to measure up to the standards set for me. What I would have given to live my life over! What I would have given to find favor in Jesus' eyes!

This time, I fell willingly to my knees before Him and asked, "Is there no way to atone for my wicked ways? Is there no way to erase the grief I have caused You?" He replied, "I require only that you confess your sins, that you be truly repentant and that you ask for My forgiveness".

I said, "But, Jesus, most of my sins were against other people. Must I not also ask for their forgiveness?" He answered in a slow voice filled with sadness, "I gave my blood for your sins so all sins are against Me....and My forgiveness is complete". I cried, "Then I do confess my sins, I am truly repentant and I humbly ask for your forgiveness".

He answered, "Rise, then, and witness your own redemption before God. Do you accept Me as your Redeemer and do you believe in the Trinity-Father, Son and Holy Spirit?" I said, "Yes, I do".

Directing my gaze toward the sky, He said, "I forgive you." My sins of the flesh disappeared from the sky.

He repeated, "I forgive you". My sins of the mind were wiped away. A third time, He said, "I forgive you". My sins of the heart vanished.

The sky was clear. I cried with happiness and rejoicing that only a forgiven sinner can understand. My soul was free. Such a great weight had been lifted from me that I could not believe that I had survived the bearing of it. I felt incredibly light. I understood, then, how it is that Angels can fly--they have no guilt holding them down. I knew the meaning of complete fulfillment, complete release from care and worry. Finally, I was able to comprehend the power, the grace and the glory of having my sins washed away by the blood of Jesus.

He looked at me and the beauty of the smile on his face was so great, I knew Eternity would not be long enough for me to fully appreciate having seen it. Then He said, "The time has not yet come for you to be presented before God. You are Not Yet Ready to enter the Kingdom of Heaven".

My soul shrank within me. A dread filled me. With a trembling voice, I asked, "Lord, please, I beg Your mercy. Take me in". He replied, "I cannot. You have work yet to be done in your mortal existence. There is more for you to do". I begged, "What is it? Let it be done, now. You have the power. Don't send me back".

I heard Him say, "You must go back. Go back".

My surroundings started fading away. A swirl of mist enveloped me. I was losing the presence of my Savior. I was fighting to hold on to something that I already knew I could not keep. I struggled mightily, then I was awakened.

Awakened??? Had it all been only a dream? Surely not. I felt such a terrible sense of loss, of emptiness. The loneliness I felt was almost unbearable. I was back inside this shell of a human body and I felt confined in a way that didn't seem possible. Trapped.

I wonder about what deeds I must do. What awaits me? What tasks are involved? Is it to be a single act or a series of acts? Am I to be a small part of a chain in a set of circumstances which will have some great (or small) impact on the world? Or am I just intended to live out my life, getting by as best I can, spending time with my family when possible, helping my friends (or strangers) when necessary and just doing what has to be done in my daily life, not knowing the day or the hour when I will be called a final time?

I hope that I will then have no regrets, no unfinished business, no tasks yet to be done. Also, I hope that, when my time comes, I will not have become so reattached to this miserable mortal existence that I will be tempted to say, "Give me a little more time, Lord, for I am Not Yet Ready".

Chapter 88

My Obituary

I was born on 9 October 1947 in Atkins, Arkansas. I am preceded in death by my parents, Steve and Alta Laverne Morris; by a brother, Cecil Ray Morris; by my infant daughter, Brandie Lynn Morris; by my step-niece, Lisa Ann Henderson Reed; by my infant niece, Jessica Marie Morris; by my infant great-niece, Ashley Rose Harelson.

I am survived by a brother and sister-in-law, E. Ray and Jannie Morris of Russellville; a sister and brother-in-law, Shirley and Dennis Henderson of Dover; a brother and sister-in-law, Steve Junior and Sherry Morris of Gravel Hill; two brothers, Robert and Danny, both of Atkins; six nieces, Jo Quinn of Perryville; Gini Harelson of Russellville; Laura Walker of Gunnison, Colorado; Renea Morris of Gravel Hill; Diana Morris of Dover; and Rachel Morris of Dover; two nephews, Jason Eubanks of Adona; and Matthew Morris of Dover; four great-nieces, Jessica Parham; Amy Eubanks; Lacy Cheyenne Harelson; and Savana Grace Harelson; two great-nephews, Jared Eubanks; and Dustin Caudell; two great-great nieces, Jaden Taylor Parham; and Austin Lane Parham; by one great-great-nephew, Tyler Bradley Parham.

I was a semi-retired farm laborer.

I was not currently a member of an established church but I always considered Sweet Home Free Will Baptist Church in the Economy community, a few miles northeast of Atkins to be my home church.

There will be no visitation, no memorial service and no funeral ceremony. My body will be cremated without the use of a casket and my ashes will be disposed of privately by E. Ray Morris, at an undisclosed place and time.

That's all I want. I don't want any mention of my marriage history, of my former employment history or of my military background. Of course, I can't enforce any of these requests and I can't dictate how my obituary will read. But these are my wishes and they seem reasonable, at least to me. I hope my wishes will be honored.

www.ingramcontent.com/pod-product-compliance
Lightning Source LLC
Chambersburg PA
CBHW051951090426

42741CB00008B/1346